GOD IS GOOD
ALL THE TIME

To John:
Blessings!
Ken Barker
(Phil. 1:20-21)

GOD IS GOOD
ALL THE TIME

My Life
a personal testimony

Kenneth L. Barker

credo
house publishers

God Is Good All the Time

Published by Credo House Publishers, a division of
Credo Communications, LLC, Grand Rapids, Michigan;
www.credohousepublishers.com.

ISBN: 978-1-625860-40-8

Cover and interior design by Nicolas Mulder

Printed in the United States of America

First Edition

To
My wife, Isabelle;
My children and their spouses: Ken and Brenda, Pat and John, Ruth and Mike, David and Dhey;
My 19 grandchildren, 9 great-grandchildren, and 1 great-great-grandson;
All who have helped to make me what I am today by God's grace;
And, most important, my Lord and Savior, Jesus Christ;
With much love and gratitude (Psalms 127–128)

CONTENTS

Chapter One

TWO BIRTHS

Is God *really* good *all* the time? One of my aims in writing this little work is to demonstrate the validity of its title: God Is Good All the Time (in spite of the bad days!). My earnest prayer is that others will be encouraged as they see how God has guided, provided, helped and blessed in my life in every way truly needed.

My opening prayer:

> Dear Lord and Heavenly Father, by the power of your Spirit enable me not only to *worship* you in all your holiness but also to *grow* in holiness and in the grace and knowledge of my Lord and Savior, Jesus Christ, and to become more and more conformed to the image of your Son in his moral and ethical character and thus in his holiness. May Christ be exalted and glorified through the words that follow in this small book, and may his goodness and all-sufficient grace be magnified.
>
> In his name, Amen.

> "By the grace of God I am what I am…not I, but the grace of God that was with me"
>
> (1 Corinthians 15:10).

When I reminisce about the life God has given me, my sentiment is the same as that of the apostle Paul: It is only by God's grace that I am what I am! I have never desired to keep a diary or journal or to write a complete autobiography (see, for instance, the biographical sketch in Appendix 1). Now that I have reached the age of 84 (as of August 13, 2015), however, I feel that it might be of some benefit and encouragement to other Christians if I would at least record selected anecdotes from some of my life experiences that, in my opinion, can only be fully explained as supernatural acts of God's grace—all glory and praise be to him alone!

To begin at the beginning, I was born the first time on August 13, 1931, in what the federal government regarded as one of the most impoverished sections of the United States, namely, the Appalachian region, specifically the hills of southeastern Kentucky at Darfork, a small coal-mining camp or community three miles from Hazard in Perry County. So I knew what poverty was like in those early, formative years. Then, too, I am the product of a broken home, for my mother and father divorced when I was only one year old. Mother raised my older brother, Herby, and me, but then she died when I was 16, leaving me virtually on my own since that age, though I lived with grandparents for a while.

Fortunately, Mother became a Christian shortly after the divorce, so I had the privilege, blessing and advantage of being raised by a godly, praying mother. Later, my father, Herbert Barker, also trusted in Christ for salvation. (I think I was about 14 years old when that happened.) Between those two conversions to Christ, Mother, Herby, and I moved to Fairfield, Connecticut, so she could get a better job on an assembly line at a manufacturing plant in Bridgeport,

Connecticut, during World War II. (I was 11 years old at the time of the move.) But when she died there five years later, it necessitated that Herby and I move back to Kentucky to live with grandparents awhile.

Back in Kentucky my father, who had become an avid witness for Christ by that time, persuaded me to go to a Youth for Christ rally at the Hazard High School auditorium to hear Coy Turner, an evangelist, on October 2, 1948. During the meeting I was under such deep conviction from the Holy Spirit that when the invitation was given, I was the first of about a dozen to go forward to receive Christ as my Savior by faith. The Holy Spirit gave me an inner compulsion that for me this decision would also entail serving Christ in a vocational sense. So I was born the second time, through a spiritual new birth, at age 17.

I am happy to report that shortly after those initial conversions of Barkers to Christ, the Holy Spirit used them to start a chain reaction among the four or five living generations of our particular Barker clan, so that within a period of just a few years, probably 95 percent of us had become Christians—Christ be praised and glorified! Most of them have been relocated from earth to heaven since then, but I still have several surviving Christian cousins in Kentucky whom I like to visit at least every other year.

Although Mother did not live to see me commit my life to Christ, I believe that the old gospel song, "Mother's Prayers Have Followed Me," is true in my case. From that moment on, the whole course of my life was radically altered and redirected, and I found security at last in Christ. I began to learn that God, or completely trusting in the God of the Holy Scriptures in and for everything, is my only real security.

Why am I writing this little book? In addition to the reason stated in the opening paragraph, I also write it for two more main reasons. First and foremost, it is my way of thanking and praising my Lord and Savior, Jesus Christ, for all *he* has done for me. It is a tribute to *him* and *his* faithful love and unfailing grace. It could also be called a testimonial concerning the radical difference Christ has made in my life. In fact, my constant prayer is the same as that of Richard of Chichester:

> To know Jesus Christ more clearly,
> To love him more dearly,
> And to follow him more nearly.

Second, I hope the Lord will use it to encourage other Christian pilgrims on their way to the Celestial City (to borrow some words from John Bunyan's *Pilgrim's Progress*). Basically, what I have attempted to accomplish in this book is to put into practice such passages of Scripture as the following (note the italicized words):

Psalm 9:1
I will give thanks to you, LORD, with all my heart;
I will tell of all your wonderful deeds.

Psalm 66:16
Come and hear, all you who fear God;
let me tell you what he has done for me.

Psalm 71:15-19
My mouth will tell of your righteous deeds,
of your saving acts all day long—
though I know not how to relate them all.
I will come and proclaim your mighty acts, Sovereign LORD;
I will proclaim your righteous deeds, yours alone.
Since my youth, God, you have taught me,
and to this day I declare your marvelous deeds.
Even when I am old and gray [as I am now],
do not forsake me, my God,
till I declare your power to the next generation,
your mighty acts to all who are to come.

Your righteousness, God, reaches to the heavens,
you who have done great things.
Who is like you, God?

Psalm 73:28
But as for me, it is good to be near God.
I have made the Sovereign Lord my refuge;
I will tell of all your deeds.

Psalm 118:15-17
Shouts of joy and victory
resound in the tents of the righteous:
The Lord's right hand has done mighty things!
The Lord's right hand is lifted high;
the Lord's right hand has done mighty things!
I will not die but live,
and will proclaim what the Lord has done.

Isaiah 12:4-5
Give praise to the Lord, call on his name;
make known among the nations what he has done,
and proclaim that his name is exalted.
Sing to the Lord, *for he has done glorious things;*
let this be known to all the world.

Isaiah 26:12
Lord, you have established peace for us;
all that we have accomplished you have done for us.

So this book is my way of "[ascribing] to the Lord the glory due his name" (Psalm 96:8). He alone deserves all the credit, honor, thanks, glory and praise for whatever *he* has enabled me to accomplish. If at times it appears that I am ascribing a little glory to myself in some of these personal illustrations, please forgive me, for that is definitely *not* my intention. My *sole* desire is to magnify God's grace.

Andraé Crouch's popular song, "My Tribute," captures my sincere desire very nicely:

How can I say thanks
For the things You have done for me—
Things so undeserved, yet You give
To prove Your love for me?
The voices of a million angels
Could not express my gratitude—
All that I am and ever hope to be,
I owe it all to Thee.

Chorus
To God be the glory,
To God be the glory!
To God be the glory
For the things He has done.
With His blood He has saved me;
With His power He has raised me;
To God be the glory
For the things he has done.

Just let me live my life—
Let it be pleasing, Lord, to Thee.
And should I gain any praise,
Let it go to Calvary.
With His blood He has saved me;
With His power He has raised me;
To God be the glory
For the things he has done.

I am in complete agreement with Paul's commitment in Romans 15:17-18: "Therefore I glory in Christ Jesus in my service to God. I will not venture to speak of anything except what Christ has accomplished through me."

My chief desire, then, is that others will come to know the same wonderful Savior I know, love and serve. As Elisha A. Hoffman expresses it in the hymn, "What a Wonderful Savior":

Christ has for sin atonement made—
What a wonderful Savior!
We are redeemed, the price is paid—
What a wonderful Savior!

I praise Him for the cleansing blood—
What a wonderful Savior!
That reconciled my soul to God—
What a wonderful Savior!

He cleansed my heart from all its sin—
What a wonderful Savior!
And now He reigns and rules therein—
What a wonderful Savior!

He gives me overcoming power—
What a wonderful Savior!
And triumph in each trying hour—
What a wonderful Savior!

Refrain
What a wonderful Savior is Jesus, my Jesus!
What a wonderful Savior is Jesus, my Lord!

"By the grace of God I am what I am."

Chapter Two

FOUR AMBITIONS

It was after the move to Fairfield, Connecticut, that I acquired my first ambition. My brother, Herby, who is 18 months older than I am, joined the Civil Air Patrol and, as soon as I was old enough, I also joined. That led to the ambition to become a pilot, first in the United States Air Force, then for a commercial airline. In preparation for the fulfillment of that desire, I completed all the requisite ground training, including navigation and meteorology. All that remained was to take flight lessons, but Mother's death brought an abrupt halt to that ambition.

Since music has always been one of my favorite hobbies or enjoyable sidelines, I joined the acapella choir at Roger Ludlowe High School in Fairfield. I had already sung the part of the captain in Gilbert and Sullivan's *H.M.S. Pinafore* operetta, presented by members of my eighth-grade class. I also sang at dances and in high school assemblies. Our director of the acapella choir informed me that she would attempt to arrange for me to try out for the Arthur Godfrey radio talent show in New York City. That led to my second ambition, namely, to become a pop singer. Again, Mother's sudden death ended those plans (but see Chapter Seven).

Mother's death (January 11, 1948—I was 16 years old) made it necessary for Herby and me to return to Kentucky and live with Grandma and Grandpa Barker in Darfork (near Hazard), at least for a year or two. There I heard about tryouts for the Hazard American Legion Junior Baseball Team (I had played a lot of amateur or sandlot baseball in Fairfield). I was planning to try out for either outfielder or pitcher, but the coach, or manager (Lus Oxley), was having difficulty finding a suitable catcher. So he announced that he was going to let each of us catch a few pitches from our star fastball pitcher until he was satisfied with one of us as his catcher. When my turn came, I kept my eyes on the ball, caught every pitch, and didn't flinch when the batter swung. The manager asked me if I had ever caught before. When I said no, he replied, "Then you are a natural-born catcher," and announced that he had found the team's catcher.

In addition to playing other American Legion Junior baseball teams, our manager also arranged for us to play in a semiprofessional league. We won first place in that league and, later, one of the two pitchers I caught made it as high as the AAA level (right next to the major leagues). Our manager told me that, after the next season (when I would be 18), he would arrange a tryout for me to play on a minor league team. That led to my third ambition—to play professional baseball as a catcher.

The Lord, however, had other plans for me. On October 2, 1948, at age 17, I invited Christ into my heart and life, and fully committed my life to him (see Chapter One). He then led me to my fourth and final ambition by giving me an inner compulsion (a "call") that I was to make myself available to serve him vocationally (in what is sometimes referred to as full-time Christian service) wherever and in whatever ways he might choose. So I began to prepare myself to bring this fourth and last ambition to fruition.

"By the grace of God I am what I am."

Chapter Three

SCHOOLS

Obviously education plays a significant and vital role in anyone's preparation for a life mission. Shortly after I trusted in Christ for salvation, I was baptized in the baptistry of First Baptist Church in Hazard, Kentucky, during a Sunday evening service. The music that evening was provided by the Challengers Quartet from Southland Bible Institute (SBI) in Pikeville (actually it was in Wolfpit, but Pikeville was the nearest fairly large post office; today the school is located near Ashland, Kentucky).

One day, after my conversion to Christ, I was walking down the hill from Hazard High School (where I was now a student) and had a most profound spiritual experience under some trees. The Lord overwhelmed me with an acute sense of his divine presence right there with me. Tears of joy filled my eyes. Although I heard no audible voice, the Lord strongly impressed upon my mind that I was to enroll at SBI for the spring quarter (though I would have the equivalent of only two years of high school at the end of the fall semester—Mother's death and the move back to Kentucky had caused me to miss a full semester).

It wasn't long after matriculating at SBI that I became

convinced that the Lord had definitely led me there—I was there in his will. I still look back on my days at SBI as the time when I was furnished with a basic foundation in Bible doctrine and the spiritual life. I particularly appreciated the emphasis on practical training in Christian service. Through SBI the Lord gave me what I needed most in those early formative years of my Christian life. The same goes for Isabelle (the Lord gave me a wonderful wife through SBI, for that is where I met her as a fellow student). She and I will always be grateful for the preparation we received there. Isabelle sang alto in the ladies' trio, and I sang the second tenor part in the Southland Quartet during our student days together there.

After I had taken classes at SBI for a year and a quarter, my friend Jerome Noble (who had also been converted to Christ through the evangelistic ministry of Coy Turner) told me about a school in Chicago (the Academy for Adults) where I could take accelerated courses and complete my last two years of high school in only nine months. He was already taking classes there and wanted me to join him. Since I knew that at some point in the near future I would need to get a high school diploma, this seemed like a good way and time to do so. The courses there were validated by examinations administered by the University of Illinois, which means that my high school diploma is actually from that university.

After the one-year interruption in my studies at SBI in order to complete my high school education, I returned to SBI to finish their three-year certificate program in my remaining two years. While doing that, a faculty member at SBI told me that a good Christian college where I could earn my B.A. degree would be Northwestern College in Minneapolis (now in St. Paul). When I discovered that they would give me two years of transfer credit for my three years at SBI, I decided to take advantage of this opportunity to earn a B.A. degree in just two more years.

Isabelle and I got married on September 5, 1953 (I was 22

years old at the time, and she was 21). While I took classes at Northwestern, she worked at the Billy Graham Evangelistic Association until I graduated two years later in 1955. (You may recall hearing on the Hour of Decision radio broadcast: "That's all the address you need—just Billy Graham, Minneapolis, Minnesota." That's where Isabelle worked.)

Two of my favorite professors at Northwestern were Drs. Terry Hulbert and Paul Haik. I took two years of Greek under Dr. Hulbert and a course in Biblical Archaeology under Dr. Haik. What impressed me most about them was their knowledge of Scripture and their ability to "correctly handle the word of truth" (2 Timothy 2:15). When I asked them where they received their theological degrees, they indicated it was Dallas Theological Seminary. They further indicated that if I wanted to become an expositor of the sacred text of Scripture itself (where one starts with a passage, stays with that passage, and finishes with that same passage), Dallas was the place to go. Since that kind of expository approach to the Biblical text was precisely what I was most interested in, I took Drs. Hulbert's and Haik's words as the Lord telling me I should go next to Dallas.

Unquestionably, Dallas Seminary exerted the greatest influence on my life and ministry—academically, intellectually, hermeneutically, exegetically, theologically, methodologically, spiritually, socially, and in every way. Some of my favorite professors there were Drs. Dwight Wayne Young (Hebrew), S. Lewis Johnson (Greek), Charles Ryrie (Theology), J. Dwight Pentecost (Bible Exposition), Donald K. Campbell (Bible), and Howard G. Hendricks (Christian Education).

It was at Dallas where the Lord made clear to me that my primary spiritual gift was teaching and I should prepare myself to equip others to serve Christ as pastors, teachers, missionaries, etc. I can honestly say that there is nothing I enjoy more than teaching and applying the text of Scripture. Since I loved Hebrew more than any of my other courses, I interpreted that as signifying that I should earn a Ph.D. in Hebrew and Old Testament Studies and teach in that area of specialization—but where could I pursue such a doctoral program of study? Since my favorite Hebrew professor (Dr. Dwight Wayne Young) had earned his doctorate at the Dropsie College for Hebrew and Cognate Learning in Philadelphia, I applied to that same institution and was accepted with a tuition-free scholarship. (After my first year there, I also became a Fellow of the College.)

Dropsie was a Jewish graduate institution offering only M.A. and Ph.D. degrees in various fields of study. In the Ph.D. program, one had to select a major and two minors. For my major, I chose Assyriology (basically the study of the cuneiform languages and literatures of ancient Assyria and Babylonia) because I wanted to major under Dr. Moshe Held, the professor in that department. (I had been encouraged to major under Dr. Held by my good friend, Ron Youngblood [now with the Lord], who was already a student there majoring in that same department.) For my minors, I selected Biblical Literature (Dr. Frank Zimmerman) and Hebrew Language and Literature (Dr. William Chomsky). It was from Dr. Held that I learned to analyze and understand all the grammatical, syntactical, and lexical details and minutiae of Semitic words and forms. The knowledge and analytical ability I gained from him equipped me to be a more effective teacher of Hebrew and other Semitic languages and literatures (see Appendix 2).

"By the grace of God I am what I am."

Chapter Four

WORK

Some may wonder where the money came from to support me (and later my entire family) during all those years of my education. The brief answer is: I earned it the old-fashioned way through hard work. I literally worked my way through all my schooling. Isabelle also worked during my two years at Northwestern College—she worked at the Billy Graham Evangelistic Association before we had our first child, Ken. (She did not work outside the home again until many years later—after our fourth and last child, David, was in school all day. Then she resumed working, part time at first, then full time for over 20 years at J.C. Penney, from which she retired.) In addition, when Mother died, my father sent me $10.00 per month. An uncle (Dr. Denzil Barker, a medical doctor in Hindman, Kentucky) likewise mailed $10.00 to me every month, specifically to help defray some of the expenses of my education. Naturally, we had to sacrifice a lot and do without many things that aren't essential anyway.

Over the years, I was involved in a variety of part-time jobs. At around age ten, I became a newspaper boy, delivering the *Hazard Herald*, which was published in Hazard, Kentucky. In Fairfield, Connecticut (during the years 1942-1948), I also delivered newspapers there, pumped gas at a service station (as well as put air in tires, added oil to motors, poured water in radiators, cleaned windshields—obviously this took place when there were still full-service gas stations [and no self-service stations!]—and cleaned the restrooms), served as assistant to the gardener on a wealthy lady's estate, and helped assemble bicycles in a bicycle manufacturing plant. Of course, these jobs were done at different times, not simultaneously.

When Herby and I moved back to Kentucky in 1948 (after Mother's death), I spent two summers driving a milk truck to deliver milk to stores (while I was a student at Southland Bible Institute). During my studies at the Academy for Adults to finish high school in Chicago, I worked part time on an assembly line in a manufacturing company. During my student days at Northwestern College for two years (1953-1955), I worked for a while at Keljik's Oriental Rugs, then in a machine shop to operate presses that used dies to make and shape various metal parts. Occasionally, I cut a hand or finger in handling the sheet metal (but at least I never lost a finger in the machines as a few of the other workers did!).

When I was a student at Dallas Seminary (1955-1959) and at the Dropsie College for Hebrew and Cognate Learning in Philadelphia (1959-1964), I worked for American Airlines as a reservations agent. Isabelle, our children, and I enjoyed all the free flights we took on American (an employee fringe benefit), though we did have to pay a small service fee. Finally, in the autumn of 1964, I began teaching at Northwestern College—my first full-time position! So you see, I had very diverse work experiences. In testimony to

God's grace, we never went hungry (though at times we ate quite a few cheap boxes of Kraft Macaroni and Cheese!). We paid all bills for rent, utilities, and the necessities of life. In short, the Lord graciously provided everything we really needed.

"By the grace of God I am what I am."

Chapter Five

ANSWERS TO PRAYER

Prayer also played a vital role in meeting our material and spiritual needs. The most important prayer I ever prayed, of course, was the one in which I invited Christ into my heart and life to be my Savior. Obviously that prayer was answered. Then I told him I was committing my life fully to him as my Lord and Master and King and was making myself available to him to be used in his service, however and wherever he may choose.

Since then, we have experienced numerous other remarkable answers to prayer. I have selected four to describe briefly.

First, while I was a student at Southland Bible Institute (SBI), our acapella quartet (I blew the pitch pipe) occasionally went with Rev. Joe Otteson (the president) for a weekend of ministry. Before leaving on such weekend ministry trips, we prayed for safe travel. That would become especially apropos on our way back to the school from a particular trip. After a Sunday evening service, Mr. Otteson was driving his car, I was in the front seat with him, and the other three quartet members were asleep in the back seat. Probably around midnight, with still at least another hour's drive left to arrive back at SBI, Mr. Otteson suddenly pulled over to the side of the road and said, "Ken, I think maybe you should drive the rest of the way. I have been asleep, because I just now woke up and don't remember anything since driving through [here he named a certain town, but I don't recall its name]." I do recall that the town he named was several miles back and, in the meantime, he had been driving on a narrow, winding mountainous road. The only explanation I have for what happened is that the Lord took control of the wheel—or sent an angel to do so—until Mr. Otteson woke up. Naturally, I responded to his offer, "Yes, I would like to drive the rest of the way back"—while praising the Lord for his protection! After all, we could easily have been killed in an accident, but the Lord wasn't finished with us yet.

Second, near the end of my last year as a student at Northwestern College, we were packing to leave for Dallas Seminary. Incidentally, Isabelle was now pregnant with our first of four children (a son, Ken). People would ask me, "Do you have a place to live?" "Do you have a job?" When I would say no, they would respond, "We think it's crazy to move with a pregnant wife to a city where you have no place to live, no friends there and no job." I would simply smile and answer, "We have prayed about it and believe that this is what the Lord wants us to do next, so we are trusting him to guide and provide."

When we arrived in Dallas in the summer of 1955, we went first to the main seminary office and inquired whether they knew of a place where we could stay until I could find an apartment or house to rent. A lady at the office informed us that we could stay in one of the seminary's guest rooms for three days at $3.00 per night. I said to God (silently), "Thank you, Lord."

Next, I went to the seminary's student bulletin board and noticed an announcement that the Federal Housing Authority had just completed George Loving Place, with two or three units of row houses set aside for students and that the rent was based on income (the lower the income, the lower the rent). We applied and were accepted and were the first occupants of our particular row house.

But now we needed furniture. So I returned to the seminary bulletin board and observed an emergency announcement by a student who had to sell all his used furniture immediately and rush back home to El Paso. He was so desperate to return to his home there as soon as possible that he was willing to let us have his whole houseful of furniture for about $200.00, which nearly depleted our small reserves. So I rented a U-Haul truck and moved the furniture into our new house.

Next, I needed a job. Once again I spotted an ad on the seminary bulletin board from the Internal Revenue Service saying they needed someone to do clerical-type work at their office in downtown Dallas. So I applied, and they indicated that I would hear from them in a few days. Meanwhile, I had met Cliff Dunlop, a dental student who lived just across from our row house in the parallel unit. He informed me that he had seen an ad on their dental school's bulletin board saying that the American Airlines reservations department (located at Amon Carter Field at that time) needed two part-time workers to work Monday-Friday from 5:00 to 9:00 pm. That would fit our class schedules, and we could carpool. We applied, and they indicated that they would contact us in a few days. A few days later, Cliff told me that we were the two applicants AA wanted, so he phoned them that we would take those two jobs. Once again, I thanked the Lord for answered prayer. Later that same day, the IRS phoned and also offered me a job, but I had to tell them that I had already made a commitment to AA. My work at AA turned out to be a very pleasant experience for nine years (four years while I was a student at DTS and five years while I studied and taught at Dropsie). After that, of course, I began teaching full time.

Third, in my first year as a student at DTS, I discovered that the Systematic Theology Department required the students to purchase Lewis Sperry Chafer's eight-volume Systematic Theology as the main textbook for all the theology courses. Unfortunately, due to all the financial drain and strain on our budget (see above), I didn't have the money to buy the whole set. So I prayed and told the Lord that if it was his will for me to purchase that set, I was trusting in him to provide the means to make it possible. Shortly after that, I received a check in the mail from my uncle (Dr. Denzil Barker again) for the exact amount needed to purchase the set—just in time to do the first reading assignment.

Fourth, while teaching at Northwestern College, near the beginning of my second year on the faculty there, the Dean announced to the faculty that, due to declining enrollment and fewer donors, the school would close at the end of the current school year. He further indicated that he was even granting permission for faculty members to *miss classes* if they needed to do so in order to have interviews elsewhere. I knew I would not feel comfortable doing that because I took my teaching responsibility there as a sacred trust or stewardship from the Lord—a stewardship that I must discharge faithfully. Besides, I wanted to give the current students their full money's worth, and to me that meant *not* missing any classes. Moreover, I firmly believed that if I was faithful in doing what the Lord had brought me there to do, I could trust in him to provide whatever new ministry opportunity he had in mind for me. And that is basically what I confided to the Lord in prayer.

Near the beginning of the second and last semester, the Dean bumped into me in the hall and inquired whether I had missed any classes to go to some interviews. When I told him no and shared with him my sentiments as written in the previous paragraph, he responded, "It sounds like good Calvinism to me," to which I replied, "Actually, Paul was a Calvinist long before Calvin was born" (my way of referring to Paul's doctrine of God's sovereignty and providence in such passages as Romans 8:28-30 and Romans 9-11). I can honestly say that I was not surprised (I was humbly grateful, but not surprised) when, near the end of that final semester, I received a phone call from Dr. Kenneth Kantzer telling me that they had an emergency need for a professor of Hebrew at Trinity Evangelical Divinity School in Deerfield, Illinois. A young instructor in that department had decided at the last minute to pursue a Ph.D. degree at New York University. When I went to Deerfield for the interview, I was satisfied with the results and they likewise seemed to be pleased. So they extended the invitation to come, and I said yes—interpreting this new teaching ministry opportunity as the Lord's leading and provision in answer to prayer. (Incidentally, I am happy to report that Northwestern is back in operation again and is growing and thriving—only now in St. Paul [actually Roseville] on beautiful Lake Johanna. The school also has a new name: University of Northwestern—St. Paul).

Many more examples of answered prayer could be given (e.g., how the Lord, in answer to the prayers of literally thousands, stabilized my grandson, Samuel, by causing a bone marrow transplant to work for his leukemia and save his life; also how the Lord caused the bones in my broken hip to finally form a complete union in answer to prayer—see Chapter Nine), but these should suffice to demonstrate the efficacy of prayer. "The prayer of a righteous person is powerful and effective" (James 5:16). Some of the reasons we Christians don't experience more such answers to prayer include these:

1. We are praying with unconfessed sin in our lives. "Your sins have hidden [God's] face from you, so that he will not hear" (Isaiah 59:2; see also Psalm 66:18; Proverbs 28:13; 1 John 1:9).

2. We are not praying in faith. "If you believe, you will receive whatever you ask for in prayer" (Matthew 21:22; see James 1:5-8).
3. We are not praying according to God's will. "This is the confidence we have in approaching God: that if we ask anything according to his will, he hears us. And if we know that he hears us—whatever we ask—we know that we have what we asked of him" (1 John 5:14-15; see Luke 22:42).
4. We are praying with wrong motives. "When you ask, you do not receive, because you ask with wrong motives, that you may spend what you get on your pleasures" (James 4:3).
5. We are not praying "in [Jesus'] name" (John 15:16). But what does it mean to pray "in [Jesus'] Name"? It is "not simply prayer that mentions Jesus' name [as at the end of a prayer: 'In Jesus' name, Amen'], but prayer in accordance with all that the person who bears the name is… It is prayer aimed at carrying forward the work Jesus did—prayer that he himself will answer" (*NIV Study Bible* note on John 14:13). It is not a blank check that we merely fill in out of selfish greed. Rather, it is praying for things that will promote the interests of Christ and will further enhance and advance the cause of his church and kingdom. The whole purpose of such praying is not to satisfy our personal desires or our own agenda, but "so that the Father may be glorified in the Son" (John 14:13). To even attempt to manipulate God through selfish prayer is an abuse and misuse of all the above passages of Scripture.

Psalm 37:4 is similarly abused and misapplied by some: "Take delight in the LORD, and he will give you the desires of your heart." "He will give you the desires of your heart" is not an Aladdin's lamp that we can rub and a divine genie appears to grant us anything we desire. What, then, is the true sense? The first part of this verse is an implied condition that must be met if we are to experience the fulfillment of the last part. If we truly take delight in the Lord, we will choose and delight in what the *Lord* chooses and delights in. Then he can give us the desires of our heart because our desires coincide with his.

Ralph S. Cushman reminds us of the importance of starting the day with God in prayer in his poem "The Secret" (though I have also seen it referred to as "I Met God in the Morning"):

I met God in the morning
When the day was at its best.
His presence came like sunrise,
Like a glory in my breast.

All day long His presence lingered,
All day long He stayed with me;
And we sailed with perfect calmness
O'er a very troubled sea.

Other ships were blown and battered,
Other ships were sore distressed;
But the wind that seemed to drive them
Brought to us a peace and rest.

Then I thought of other mornings
With a keen remorse of mind,
When I, too, had loosed the moorings
With His presence left behind.

So I think I know the secret,
Learned from many a troubled way;
You must meet God in the morning
If you want Him through the day.

Two brief anonymous poems add a touch of humor to the subject of prayer yet still stress its importance:

We mutter and sputter,
We fume and we spurt,
We mumble and grumble,
Our feelings get hurt;
We can't understand things,
Our vision grows dim,
When all that we need
Is a moment with Him.

Overheard in an Orchard
Said the Robin to the Sparrow,
"I should really like to know
Why those anxious human beings
Rush about and worry so."

Said the Sparrow to the Robin,
"Friend, I think that it must be
That they have no Heavenly Father
Such as cares for you and me."

A fairly frequent prayer pattern of mine goes something like this (though the words vary from time to time):

Dear Lord and Heavenly Father,

I love you, thank you, and praise you for all that you are, all that you do, and all that you provide. I worship you for your marvelous attributes and all the ways you reveal, manifest, and express those attributes to me and my extended family—such as your great love, grace, faithfulness, mercy and forgiveness. May your Spirit enable me to always be a usable instrument in your hands, carrying out your will as your faithful and humble servant—all to your glory.

In Jesus' name, Amen.

So be encouraged to persevere in prayer and faith by these words from C.A. Gabriel:

Pray when the storm-clouds gather o'er-head,
Hiding the light from you,
Filling your soul with darkness and dread,
Pray till the light breaks through.

Pray then believing, God on the throne
Looks with compassion true
Unto His children, cares for His own.
Pray till the light breaks through.

Refrain
Just keep on praying through,
The Lord will answer you;
God keeps His promise true,
Just keep on praying till light breaks through.

"By the grace of God I am what I am."

Chapter Six

TEACHING

Just as I worked at many different secular jobs and places, so I taught at several Christian educational institutions (see Appendix 2 under VOCATIONAL EXPERIENCE). I have often wondered if the reason the Lord moved me around so much by opening so many different doors of ministry for me is that I am basically a vagabond or rover by nature. I like to travel and enjoy a variety of new experiences. In fact, after serving anywhere for several years, I start getting a little "antsy" for a change.

Actually, my first teaching position was at Dropsie College in Philadelphia, where I stayed an extra year (1963-1964) to teach full time in the Department of Assyriology with Dr. Held. During that year, I received a phone call from the Dean of Northwestern College asking if I would be interested in teaching at my alma mater. Naturally I was interested since I was in my last year at Dropsie. They flew me there for an interview. That resulted in an invitation to join their faculty. I prayed for wisdom (à la James 1:5) to discern God's will. Isabelle and I both came to believe that it was his will, so I signed the contract and mailed it. Interestingly, shortly after I mailed the contract to Northwestern College, I received a letter from Dr. Bob Cook, at that time the President of the King's College in Briarcliff Manor, New York, asking if I would be interested in teaching there. Naturally, I had to write him that his invitation arrived a little too late to be considered.

I enjoyed my two years of teaching at Northwestern (1964-1966). It was my only experience in teaching at the college level. Some of the courses I taught there were New Testament Greek, Bible Study Methods, Bible Survey, Introduction to the Old Testament, History of Israel and the Gospel of Luke. During my last year at Northwestern, Dr. Ken Kantzer phoned me and asked if I would be interested in teaching at Trinity Evangelical Divinity School (see Chapter Five). Since Northwestern was closing, obviously I was interested, and the result was that I became Assistant Professor of Old Testament and Archaeology there.

I was very happy at Trinity (1966-1968) and had particularly close, pleasant, personal friendships with such evangelical leaders as Drs. Ken Kantzer, Gleason Archer, Walt Kaiser, Tom McComiskey, Dick Longenecker, Elmer Towns, David Hesselgrave, and Walt Liefield. It was a true Biblical *koinonia*—a vital "fellowship" or "partnership" in Christ, our common Lord. A few of us enjoyed kidding each other. For instance, one day as Dr. Towns (Professor of Christian Education) and his students were exiting a classroom and I and my students were waiting to enter that same classroom, he loudly asked me on his way out, "Why don't you give your students something practical?" I responded, "And why don't you give your students something with substance?"

During my second year there, Dr. John Walvoord (President of Dallas Seminary) phoned me and indicated that he would be speaking in a chapel service at Trinity on a certain date and wondered if he could meet with me in my office either before or after chapel, and the time was set. In our meeting, he asked if I would be interested in teaching at my alma mater. I told him it would be a difficult decision because I was happy at Trinity. But then Walvoord pointed out that at Dallas I could teach even more Hebrew (including Hebrew exegesis) and cognate languages. This would be more in keeping with all my graduate and postgraduate studies and preparation. So I promised Walvoord I would pray and seek the Lord's guidance in the matter. Then I asked my four children how they felt about the prospect of returning to the city where they had been born, and all of them were excited and enthusiastic about such a possibility. So after much prayer and deliberation, Isabelle and I concluded that it was indeed God's will for us to make the move to Dallas.

My thirteen years (1968-1981) on the faculty of Dallas Seminary were among the happiest and most productive of my entire life and ministry. And the administration there (especially Dr. Walvoord, President, and Dr. Donald Campbell, Dean) did everything in their power to make me happy and keep me that way. For example, they promoted me from Assistant Professor to Associate Professor to Full Professor in the minimum time possible. They also allowed me to devote considerable time to translating the NIV. For about the last half of my tenure there, I also served as Chairman of the Department of Semitics and Old Testament Studies because, when Dr. Bruce Waltke (the previous Chairman) took a sabbatical to teach at Regent College in Canada and notified Dr. Walvoord that he would not be returning, Walvoord promoted me to Chairman. During the last few years of my Chairmanship there, the Lord blessed and prospered our department so much that we grew to the point where we had more majors than any other department at the seminary. We had seven faculty members in our department alone: Walt Bodine, Don Glenn, Gene Merrill, Jackie Deere, Craig Glickman, Al Ross and, of course, myself. The Lord has given me many fond memories of the Dallas experience.

For my last stint of teaching in an academic context, we must skip from 1981 to 1986 (see the next chapter to fill in that gap). From the fall of 1986 through the spring of 1990, I served as Academic Dean and Professor of Old Testament at Capital Bible Seminary (CBS) in Lanham, Maryland, near Washington, D.C. This was my first taste of true administrative work (though I came close as Chairman of the Old Testament Department at Dallas).

One of the first things I did there was to ask the President of CBS (and Washington Bible College) to add to Dr. Todd Beall's title so that he was not only Registrar but also Assistant Dean, and to promote Wilma McMann from Secretary to Administrative Assistant. This would allow me to delegate many of the "details" and much of the "busy work" to them, thus retaining only the weightier issues for myself. It would also free me up to teach some. Besides, I have always believed in teamwork—surrounding myself with competent people and delegating some of the load to them. Dr. Beall once told me, "You are the best delegator I have ever seen." I am extremely grateful for all the members of the CBS administration, staff, faculty, and student body, as well as for all the valuable experiences the Lord gave me there. On May 19, 2007, at the invitation of President Larry Mercer, I was able to return and deliver the Commencement address there.

It has been a priceless, awesome and humbling privilege, joy and blessing to teach so many wonderful students over the years. Here is a partial list of some of the more well-known former students of mine:

From Dropsie: David Marcus

From Trinity: Rick Melick, Carl Rasmussen, Ed Hindson

From Dallas: Paul Tanner, Ken Mathews, Ellis Brotzman, Ron Allen, Al Ross, Tommy Ice, Greg Beale, Scott Rae, Bud (Ray) Ortlund, Darrell Bock, Dan Wallace, Buist Fanning, Bob Chisholm, Michael Harbin, Ray Clendenen,

Mark Rooker, Tony Evans, Tim Timmons, George Nicewonger, Ken Gire, J.P. Moreland, Rex Koivisto, Paul Enns, Hall Harris, Steve Westfall, Mark Littleton, John Master, Van Parunak, Greg Parsons, David Kennedy, Randall Price, Bob Wall, Steve Henderson, Craig Glickman, Doug Kennard, John Grassmick, Byang Kato, Bruce Wilkinson, Wayne Brindle, James Mook, Arnie Fruchtenbaum, Ken Boa, Paul Karleen, Mark Bailey, Scott Horrell, Ray Pritchard, Lanier Burns

From Capital: Charles Ware, Femi Adeyemi, Samuel Ekwue, Colin Smith, Beau Abernathy, Kyle Austin, Wayne Sutton, Jerry Marcellino, Olu Ijatuyi, Randy Seiver, Kelvin McCune

It is also a source of great blessing, encouragement, and satisfaction to travel throughout the country (as well as through other countries) and see how so many of my former students are making themselves available for the Lord to use them in such powerful and significant ways. It gives me a sense of great reward and fulfillment to have had even a small role in the preparation of such faithful and fruitful servants of Christ.

"By the grace of God I am what I am."

Chapter Seven

DIVERSE MINISTRIES

I have always been amazed at the variety of ministries the Lord has allowed me to be involved in. The last chapter summarized my teaching ministry in academic contexts (primarily theological seminaries). This chapter will briefly sketch several other ministries, one of which is music. I sang solos (frequently before preaching in churches) as well as in duets (including with my wife, Isabelle—we even sang a duet at our wedding!), trios, quartets, ensembles, and choirs. My main theme song for all my singing was "My Wonderful Lord" by Haldor Lillenas:

> I have found a deep peace that I never had
> known
> And a joy this world could not afford,
> Since I yielded control of my body and soul
> To my wonderful, wonderful Lord.
> I desire that my life shall be ordered by Thee,
> That my will be in perfect accord
> With thine own sov'reign will Thy desires to
> fulfill,
> My wonderful, wonderful Lord.
> Thou art fairer to me than the fairest of earth,

Thou omnipotent, life-giving Word;
O Thou Ancient of Days, Thou art worthy all praise,
My wonderful, wonderful Lord!

Chorus
My wonderful Lord, my wonderful Lord,
By angels and seraphs in heaven adored;
I bow at Thy shrine,* my Savior divine,
My wonderful, wonderful Lord.

(* Used here in the sense of a sacred place or altar of worship associated with a holy person, namely, Christ)

Shortly after I received Christ as my Savior by faith (see Chapter One), I helped form the original Barker Family Quartet. We sang at churches, camps, conferences, other special events, and on the radio. Grandpa Barker sang bass, Dad sang tenor, Jena (one of my two sisters; Ellie was the other one—both are now deceased) sang alto, and I was the lead singer. When Jena and I had to leave for school, I was replaced by Uncle Arnold, and Jena was replaced by her mother (my stepmother, Sibyl). Grandpa ("Pop") wrote several of the songs himself. Most of his songs would probably be classified today as Southern Gospel.

Pop kept a Journal, and I have a copy of part of it. You can catch a glimpse of his heart for God by reading a few selected quotations from various entries:

Entry for Dec. 31, 1943	"God always knows best."
Entry for Jan. 1, 1944	"I am praising God this New Year's morning. Please guide me, dear Lord, through 1944."
Entry for Jan. 28, 1944	"I am praising God this rainy morning. I must trust in Him for

	my two boys [Denzil and Tim] in the army [during World War II]—that He will bring them back" [He did].
Entry for Feb 1, 1944	"Lord, I am trusting in Thee, and I thank you for this beautiful day."
Entry for Feb. 4, 1944	"A cloudy morning and a cloudy world, but the sun will shine again—so happy day!"
Entry for Feb. 9, 1944	"Dear Father in heaven, thy love has kept me through the night and has opened my eyes to another new day. Help me, dear Father, to treasure this day and, although some of its hours may be dark, give me the light to live it as thou wouldst have me live."

As you can see, he was quite a man of God—as was his son, my dad.

During one of the years when I was a student at Southland Bible Institute, I had a weekly radio broadcast called "Songs from the Heart." The theme song for all these radio broadcasts was "It's in My Heart" by Arthur Slater:

> Tho' some may sing to pass the weary night along;
> Tho' some may sing to entertain a worldly throng,
> I sing because I worship God in song;
> It's in my heart; It's in my heart.
>
> You ask me how I know His blood can cleanse alone;
> You ask me how I know He sits upon the throne
> And how I know He chose me for His own;
> It's in my heart; It's in my heart.

Chorus
It's in my heart—this melody of love divine;
It's in my heart since I am His and He is mine;
It's in my heart—how can I help but sing and shine?
It's in my heart; It's in my heart.

My most frequently requested song was "Jesus the Son of God" by G. T. Haywood:

Do you know Jesus, Our Lord, our Savior,
Jesus the Son of God?
Have you ever seen Him, Or shared in His favor?
Jesus the Son of God.
If you will accept Him And trust and believe Him,
Jesus the Son of God,
Your soul will exalt Him And never will leave Him,
Jesus the Son of God.
Then some day from Heaven, On clouds of bright glory,
Jesus the Son of God
Will come for His jewels, Most precious and holy,
Jesus the Son of God.

Chorus
O sweet Wonder! O sweet Wonder!
Jesus the Son of God;
How I adore Thee! O how I love Thee!
Jesus the Son of God.

During all three years at Southland, I led and sang in the Southland Quartet. I also took a break for about nine months to travel with Evangelist Coy Turner (under whose ministry I was converted to Christ) and served as his song leader, soloist, and director of volunteer choirs in evangelistic tent meetings. When I was a student at Northwestern College, I was a song leader, soloist, and choir director (as well as Sunday School teacher) at Riverside Evangelical Free Church (Minneapolis).

Another ministry was that of teaching in non-academic settings. In my student days, I taught Sunday School and other classes at Riverside Evangelical Free Church in Minneapolis; Winnetka Bible Church in Dallas (Oak Cliff); and Berachah Church in Cheltenham, Pennsylvania (near Philadelphia). During my academic teaching years, I taught Sunday School and other classes at Riverside Evangelical Free Church (again!); North Suburban Evangelical Free Church in Deerfield, Illinois; Northwood Evangelical Free Church in north Dallas; Reinhardt Bible Church in Garland, Texas (near Dallas); and Forcey Memorial Church in Silver Spring, Maryland. When I was on the staff of International Bible Society (1981-1986 and 1990-1996), I taught Sunday School and discipleship classes at Montgomery Evangelical Free Church in Belle Meade, New Jersey; and First Baptist Church in Carrollton, Texas (I continue such a teaching ministry there in my "retirement").

In addition, I had the joy, privilege, and blessing of serving several churches as Interim Pastor: Rusk Bethel Baptist Church (American Baptist) in Menomonie, Wisconsin, 1964-1965; Riverside Evangelical Free Church in Minneapolis, 1965-1966; Irving Bible Church in Irving, Texas, 1971-1973 (18 months—I followed Chuck Swindoll there); Lubbock Bible Church in Lubbock, Texas, 1980; and the Christian and Missionary Alliance Church in Cranford, New Jersey, 1983. I was also founding Pastor of Faith Evangelical Free Church in Colts Neck, New Jersey (now relocated to suburban Freehold, New Jersey), 1985-1986.

Altogether, I have had the privilege and opportunity of serving as guest minister or Bible teacher at well over 150 churches (large, medium, and small), camps, conferences, retreats, seminars, colleges and seminaries throughout the United States, the United Kingdom, and a few other countries. These included not only independent (or interdenominational or unaffiliated) churches, but also most of the major denominations (Baptist, Presbyterian, Methodist, Episcopal, Anglican, Evangelical Free, etc.).

Still another ministry was Bible translation. What a blessing it has been to work with some of God's greatest servants in translating his Word! Most people know me as a translator of the NIV (and as General Editor of *The NIV Study Bible*), but actually the first English Bible I helped translate was the NASB (I devoted two full summers to translating part of the Old Testament of that version—the summers of 1969 and 1970).

Then, in 1971, I received a phone call from Dr. Edwin (Ed) Palmer, Executive Secretary of the NIV Committee on Bible Translation (CBT) and Coordinator of all translation work on the NIV. He told me about a new project under way to translate the Bible accurately from the original languages (Hebrew, Aramaic, and Greek) into clear, contemporary English, and invited me to join other scholars from around the world to participate in this historic venture. I listened courteously and patiently to his presentation, thanked him for inviting me—and turned him down. I told him I was extremely busy with teaching, speaking engagements, and writing and editing commitments. Besides, I wasn't sure I agreed with a translation approach that was freer than the one used in producing the more literal NASB.

But Palmer persisted and, using better psychology this time, he called me again almost one year later. He explained that a translation committee working on the book of Hosea was scheduled to meet for two weeks in St. Louis during my spring break, and he asked me to help them. If I was not satisfied with their approach, he promised never to bother me again about the NIV. But if I wanted to continue with them, they would be glad to have me. That seemed fair enough, so I went and participated. In those two weeks I became totally sold on the project. After that, I devoted all the time, energy, and money I could spare to the NIV.

In 1974, I was promoted to CBT, the 15-person governing committee that oversees all translation work on the NIV and that is responsible for the final content of the entire Biblical text, including wording and format (see Appendix 5). Shortly after that (early 1975), I was elected as CBT's Secretary (a post that also put me on CBT's Executive Committee, consisting of the Chair, the Vice-Chair and the Secretary), a position I held for almost 30 years (longer than any other CBT officer). In addition to the NIV (including its 2011 edition), I also helped translate the NIrV and the TNIV (see Appendix 3).

God has blessed our translation efforts beyond all expectations. There are now more than 400 million NIV Bibles and New Testaments in print, and thus in worldwide circulation and use. It brings me great joy to hear that people everywhere have been edified through reading and studying the NIV. For example, I received an encouraging letter from a new Christian in England. He told me that so much of the old English in the KJV went over his head that he lost interest in reading it. Then his wife gave him the NIV, and he couldn't put it down. He read it for hours at a time. That is what makes all our efforts worthwhile.

When we completed our work on the NIV in 1978, some of us began immediately to produce for Zondervan the *NIV Study Bible* (NIVSB), with book introductions, essays, study notes, maps, photos, charts, diagrams, concordance, indexes, and other helps. The original General Editor was Ed Palmer; the Old Testament Associate Editors were John Stek, Ronald Youngblood, and myself; and the New Testament Associate Editors were Donald Burdick and Walter Wessel. Unfortunately, Ed died of a heart attack in September of 1980. Within only a few weeks after that, Rev. Youngve Kindberg, President of International Bible Society (IBS, the financial sponsor of the NIV and CBT, and the organization that paid Ed's salary as the full-time Executive Secretary of CBT), phoned me and asked if he could meet with me at the Dallas-Ft. Worth International Airport for a long lunch there together, and I said yes. So he flew in to meet with me.

In our meeting, Kindberg explained that CBT, the top corporate officers at Zondervan, and the Board of IBS, were all unanimous that I should succeed Ed as Executive Secretary of CBT and General Editor of the NIVSB. Furthermore, he indicated that since my salary would come from IBS, they also wanted me to have the title, Senior Vice President of IBS. This meant that I would have to resign as Chairman of the Old Testament Department at Dallas Theological Seminary, and Isabelle and I would need to move to East Brunswick, New Jersey, the location of the headquarters of IBS at that time (now located in Colorado Springs and now called Biblica), which we did. In my capacity as Executive Secretary of CBT, I led CBT to a successful NIV revision session in the summer of 1983. In my capacity as General Editor of the NIVSB, I led my team of contributors and Associate Editors to the completion of the NIVSB in 1985—which, incidentally, has now sold over ten million copies. However, I did not feel comfortable with what IBS and Zondervan were coming up with to fill up my time beyond 1985. Moreover, I was sensing an increasing desire to return to the academic scene. That's when I was invited to become Academic Dean and Professor of Old Testament at Capital Bible Seminary (CBS), and I felt led to accept the invitation (see Chapter Six).

However, IBS was not finished with me yet. Near the end of the first semester of my fourth year at CBS (1989-1990), I received a phone call from Jim Powell, the new president of IBS, explaining that they needed someone to serve as half-time Executive Director of their new NIV Translation Center and that I was the most qualified person for this new position. Furthermore, they would move us to Colorado Springs, where I could have an office in their new headquarters building, or, if we preferred, they would move us to the location of our choice and I could operate out of an office in my home. Now it just so happens that, prior to that call, I was beginning to need more time for writing and editing commitments and this half-time ministry would provide that extra time. And both Isabelle and I had a growing desire to live close to where most of our children and grandchildren were now living and a move to Lewisville, Texas (with an office in my home), would fulfill that desire. To us, it seemed as though the Lord was saying, "You have a growing desire for more time to write and edit, as well as a desire to live close to where most of your children and grandchildren live—here it is." He dropped into our laps a way to fulfill both desires. So after prayer we concluded that this was indeed God's will for us and made the move. Incidentally, Isabelle became my secretary (they also paid her).

My new job description included the following:

1. Support *commercial* NIV publishers (IBS publishes *non-commercial* editions of the NIV) by speaking at NIV Pastors' Breakfasts sponsored by IBS, Zondervan (or Hodder & Stoughton in the United Kingdom), and local Christian bookstores, and by being available to answer questions about the NIV.
2. Answer all NIV-related correspondence within 30 days.
3. Appear on TV and radio programs as scheduled.
4. Write resource articles and books about the NIV for promotional and publication use by the media.
5. Fulfill the duties of Secretary of CBT and member of its Executive Committee.
6. Maintain contact with the theological and linguistic branches of the scholarly world to represent the evangelical viewpoint of IBS (e.g., by attending and/or presenting papers at Evangelical Theological Society [ETS] and Society of Biblical Literature [SBL] conventions).

Regarding point 1 above, I traveled throughout the United States and the United Kingdom speaking to over 10,000 pastors and other Christian leaders in well over 100 meetings.

Regarding point 2, I am happy to report that at least 90 percent of the letters I have received from people around the world have been positive, essentially thanking us for the NIV. I, in turn, wrote to thank them for such kind and encouraging words of appreciation for the NIV. Naturally, I also responded to most of the critical letters. However, I did not respond to all the criticisms. There are several reasons for this: (1) Some critics clearly had other agendas than providing a completely unbiased, objective evaluation of the NIV. (2) Many of their criticisms applied equally well to the other English versions. (3) Many of the complaints belonged in the category of nitpicking. (4) Some NIV renderings were already under review by CBT, and we needed to wait until the results were made known before commenting on those passages.

Probably I should have expected the criticisms just mentioned. The history of English Bible translation work demonstrates that whenever anyone sets out either to revise an existing English version of the Bible or to produce a new English version, there will be criticism. It seems to come with the territory. As D. Ewert (in his book *From Ancient Tablets to Modern Translations* [Grand Rapids: Zondervan, 1983], page 203) points out concerning even the KJV/AV:

> Critics accused the (KJV/AV) translators of blasphemy and modernism and called them "damnable corrupters." The AV was denounced as being unfaithful to the original, and one London clergyman thought it denied the deity of Jesus Christ.
>
> The dissenters who fled to America took the Geneva Bible with them, since in their view,

> the AV reminded them too much of the divine right of kings. Attacks on the AV continued almost to the end of the seventeenth century, but eventually this version won out over all others.

The NIV has followed a similar pattern, except that it "won out" faster than the King James Version.

Regarding point 3, I have been interviewed on TV and radio programs and by reporters from magazines and newspapers throughout the United States and the United Kingdom.

Regarding point 4, I have edited and/or written a trilogy of books about the NIV: *The Making of the NIV, The Accuracy of the NIV,* and *The Balance of the NIV.* I have also contributed chapters to books as well as articles to magazines and newspapers.

Regarding point 5, I retired as Secretary of CBT in 2004 (see Appendix 3), though I continued to chair (or moderate) its work sessions. In the summer of 2011 (when I became 80 years old), I retired from CBT—after helping to produce the 2011 edition of the NIV. However, my name will continue to be listed as an honorary member of CBT for as long as I live.

Regarding point 6, I have presented several position papers about the NIV and its translation process at the annual conventions of both ETS and SBL.

Diverse ministries also include writing commentaries on Micah for the *New American Commentary* (NAC) and on Zechariah for the *Expositor's Bible Commentary* (EBC) as well as co-editing the *EBC: Abridged Edition* (2 volumes). Finally, I have written numerous articles, book reviews, and chapters for encyclopedias, books, journals, and magazines. These diverse ministries have taken me to 25 foreign countries and all 50 states of the USA.

"By the grace of God I am what I am."

Chapter Eight

INFLUENTIAL PEOPLE

Abraham Lincoln once said, "All that I am or hope to be, I owe to my angel mother." I wish to expand this familiar saying: "All that I am or ever hope to be, I owe to my Lord and Savior, Jesus Christ, to my Grandma Barker, to my mother (Ruby) and to my wife (Isabelle). First, I owe everything to Christ: "I eagerly expect and hope that I will in no way be ashamed, but will have sufficient courage so that now as always Christ will be exalted in my body, whether by life or by death. For to me, to live is Christ and to die is gain" (Philippians 1:20-21; see also John 10:10). "I am the vine; you are the branches. If you remain in me and I in you, you will bear much fruit; apart from me you can do nothing" (John 15:5). "I have learned to be content whatever the circumstances. I know what it is to be in need, and I know what it is to have plenty. I have learned the secret of being content in any and every situation, whether well fed or hungry, whether living in plenty or in want. I can do all this through [Christ] who gives me strength" (Philippians 4:11-13).

Without Christ I can accomplish "nothing" (John 15:5), and indeed without him I am nothing! As Mylon LeFevre's song puts it:

Without Him I could do nothing,
Without Him I'd surely fail;
Without Him I would be drifting
Like a ship without a sail.

But with Christ and his all-sufficient "grace" (2 Corinthians 12:9) and "strength" (Philippians 4:13), I can cope with "any and every situation…whether living in plenty or in want" (Philippians 4:12). Now my earnest desire is "to know Christ" better (Philippians 3:10) and to make him known to others. I owe Christ so much that I want to serve him so faithfully, fruitfully, and obediently that one day I will hear his words of approbation: "Well done, good and faithful servant! You have been faithful with a few things; I will put you in charge of many things. Come and share your master's happiness!" (Matthew 25:21, 23). In any event I will say, "Worthy is the Lamb, who was slain, to receive power and wealth and wisdom and strength and honor and glory and praise" (Revelation 5:12). And if I receive any "crowns," I will join those who "lay their crowns before the throne and say: 'You are worthy, our Lord and God, to receive glory and honor and power'" (Revelation 4:10–11).

Second, I owe much to my grandmother (Grandma Barker), who became like a second mother to me. Incidentally, I never saw her lose her temper or heard her utter one unkind or harsh word about anyone. What an example!

Third, I owe a lot to my mother (Ruby Wells). As I mentioned in Chapter One, my mother and father divorced when I was one year old, so Mother had to raise my brother, Herby, and me. She worked hard to support the three of us. Fortunately, shortly after the divorce she became a Christian. She hung a plaque on the wall of the bedroom where Herby and I slept. I can still visualize the raised, polished, white letters on a blue velvet background. It read: "Do nothing that you would not like to be doing when Jesus comes; say nothing that you would not like to be saying when Jesus comes; go to no place where you would not like to be found when Jesus comes." Obviously it made an indelible impression on my mind.

Mother was a godly, praying woman. Often when I would come home from a movie date fairly late in the evening, I would find her on her knees praying at her bedside before she actually went to bed. I couldn't miss seeing her because I had to pass through her bedroom to get to mine. She didn't have to tell me for whom she was praying and for what she was praying. I knew. As I indicated at the beginning of this little book, Mother didn't live long enough to see me trust in her Savior and commit my life to him, but her prayers have been answered. The title of an old gospel song is true of me: "Mother's Prayers Have Followed Me." Obviously I am looking forward to seeing her again at our grand reunion in heaven.

Fourth, I also owe much to my loving, caring, devoted, faithful wife, Isabelle. The words of Proverbs 31: 10-13, 20, 25-31 are true of her: "A wife of noble character who can find? She is worth far more than rubies. Her husband has full confidence in her and lacks nothing of value. She brings him good, not harm, all the days of her life. She... works with eager hands. She opens her arms to the poor and extends her hands to the needy. She is clothed with strength and dignity; she can laugh at the days to come. She speaks with wisdom, and faithful instruction is on her tongue. She watches over the affairs of her household and does not eat the bread of idleness. Her children arise and call her blessed; her husband also, and he praises her: 'Many women do noble things, but you surpass them all.' Charm is deceptive, and beauty is fleeting; but a woman who fears the Lord is to be praised. Honor her for all that her hands have done, and let her works bring her praise at the city gate."

When I first saw Isabelle sing alto in a ladies trio at Southland Bible Institute (SBI), I was attracted to her. You may be interested in knowing how we started dating. SBI occasionally held picnic "outings" with recreational activities.

One activity was a three-legged race, in which my right leg was tied to her left, hence three legs. We won the race, so I suggested to her that we begin dating to see if we could *continue winning together*. To my pleasant surprise, she agreed. This year (2016) marks our 63rd wedding anniversary, so we are still winning together. To celebrate our golden (50th) anniversary, I took her on an unforgettable Alaskan cruise. I will say more about her in the next chapter (see also Appendix 3).

Other individuals the Lord has used to influence me greatly and in different ways include Bob Salstrom (in whose church in Minnesota I was the teacher at several Bible conferences, and who taught me much, by example, about the life of faith—not only about *living* by faith but also about *loving* and *giving* by faith); Grandma and Grandpa Barker (who "took me in" more than once); my father, Herb Barker (who modeled, better than anyone I know, what a balanced Christian life should look like); Floyd Sharp (who encouraged me when I needed it; see Chapter Nine); all my faculty colleagues (too many to name); my fellow Bible translators (also too many to name, but I will single out Donald J. Wiseman because I introduced him to ice cream sundaes—he loved them!); my NIVSB Associate Editors (especially Ron Youngblood, Mark Strauss, and John Stek); Dr. Jeff Panosian, a close friend with whom I am working on principles of Biblical interpretation; Joe Battino, who prays with me regularly (by phone); my pastor, Dr. Brent Taylor, who is an excellent pastor and preacher; and, of course, my four children (and their spouses) and 29 grandchildren (also too many to name), including 9 great-grandchildren and 1 great-great-grandson. Incidentally, 11 of my grandchildren are adopted from India, China, Latvia, Vietnam, Ethiopia, and the Philippines (adopted by my older son Ken and his wife Brenda). They are a much-loved part of our family.

"By the grace of God I am what I am."

Chapter Nine

GOD IS GOOD ALL THE TIME

Disappointment, discouragement, and pain come to all humans. Sometimes the pain is physical hurt; at other times it is mental and emotional hurt. I have had my share of both kinds of pain. W.B. Stevens put it like this:

> Tempted and tried we're oft made to wonder
> Why it should be thus all the day long,
> While there are others living about us
> Never molested, tho' in the wrong.
>
> When we see Jesus coming in glory,
> When He comes from His home in the sky,
> Then we shall meet Him in that bright mansion;
> We'll understand it all by and by.
>
> Chorus
> Farther along we'll know all about it,
> Farther along we'll understand why;
> Cheer up, my brother, live in the sunshine;
> We'll understand it all by and by.

John Newton brings God's grace into the picture:

> Thro' many dangers, toils and snares
> I have already come.
> 'Tis grace hath bro't me safe thus far,
> And grace will lead me home.

Andy Stanley (in *Today's Devotional Bible*, Zondervan, 2006, page 1040) reminds us that to better understand what is happening to us, we need God's perspective:

> It's amazing how much your perspective can change with a little information. As a young child, the idea of allowing a doctor to give you a shot probably didn't make much sense. In fact, it may have taken some parental pressure or bribery to get you to cooperate. You didn't know anything about preventive medicine or what immunization meant. All you knew was that it hurt.
>
> Over time, of course, things change. By the time you're an adult, you go to the doctor under your own power. You submit willingly to the same kind of shot. You even pay to have it done to you. All because information has altered your perspective.
>
> As a child of God, the same is true. God declares, "So are my ways higher than your ways…my thoughts than your thoughts" (Isaiah 55:9). No matter how old or smart you get, there are some things about life you just won't understand like God does. You don't think as God thinks because you simply don't have the information. His perspective runs across millions of years, and it leaves nothing out of the equation. He has more information than the

> human brain can hope to contain. That's why it's always better to follow God's intuition rather than our own.

Two surgeries brought the greatest *physical* pain to me: First, there was the time in early 1981 when I had to have several large hemorrhoids plus a grape-sized benign tumor surgically removed by a proctologist. My dear wife helped to nurse me back to full health and strength.

Second, there was the time at the end of November in 1997 when I fell and broke my right hip while playing with Lauren and Zack, two of my grandchildren. (Doesn't that qualify as breaking my hip for a worthy cause?) A Christian orthopedic surgeon, Dr. Bob Mendonsa, repaired the break, using three steel screws (which are still there) to press the lower part of the femur tight against the upper part (the break was just below the ball or head of the femur).

The break and the surgery were painful enough. But then there was a reflex action in my right foot called RSD (Reflex Sympathetic Dystrophy) as a result of such trauma. My foot became all swollen, discolored, and extremely sensitive. There were times when, if Isabelle would even touch it, bolts of excruciating pain would shoot through it like lightning. At one point the pain became so intense and intolerable that I prayed and even asked the Lord either to cause the pain to ease up a little or to just take me on home to pain-free heaven. Thankfully, he did cause the pain to begin to subside—slowly. He accomplished this through a physical therapist named Sandy (recommended by Dr. Mendonsa), who knew just the right therapies to cure RSD—but only if it was caught soon enough (mine was).

But that isn't the end of the story. Every three months I went to Dr. Mendonsa for follow-up x-rays to check the healing progress of my repaired hip. A good union was forming in the middle of the fracture line but not at the two ends, where there were still fairly large gaps. Finally, a little more than nine months after the accident, an x-ray in September revealed no further progress toward a complete union since the previous x-ray. So Dr. Mendonsa concluded that I may have to accept the probability that I will have only an incomplete union, but he wanted me to return for a final x-ray in December just to be certain that we should expect no further healing progress.

When I returned for that final x-ray in December, Dr. Mendonsa showed it to me with a big smile on his face and said, "Not only do you have a complete union, but I can't even detect the fracture line anymore—it's a miracle!" I responded, "I believe that, because God does hear and answer prayer. Many people have been praying for complete healing together with us, and God has answered our prayers." Dr. Mendonsa concurred. Incidentally, he also told me that the Lord used me to help draw him to Christ as his Savior and as the Lord of his life and to influence him to become an active Christian, more involved in his church instead of simply being a nominal Christian. He and his lovely family have made several medical mission trips to bring both physical and spiritual healing to the people of Kenya. He now has a remarkable testimony about how Christ has totally transformed his life.

In such times of testing as I endured by God's grace and enablement, we need to do what David did many times (see his psalms), namely, commit our problems and troubles to the Lord in prayer, trust in him and his good providence, and persevere in a life of faith, faithfulness, fruitfulness, and obedience to his will as revealed in his Word—even when it seems that everything is going wrong! When we are "tempted and tried," we need the kind of faith William H. Bathurst wrote about in his hymn, "O For a Faith That Will Not Shrink":

O for a faith that will not shrink
Though pressed by many a foe,
That will not tremble on the brink
Of any earthly woe;

That will not murmur nor complain
Beneath the chast'ning rod,
But in the hour of grief or pain
Will lean upon its God;
A faith that shines more bright and clear
When tempests rage without,
That, when in danger, knows no fear,
In darkness feels no doubt.

Lord, give me such a faith as this
And then, whate'er may come,
I'll taste e'en now the hallowed bliss
Of an eternal home.

Three experiences also brought me some *mental* and *emotional* pain. First, there were the attacks of KJV Onlyites against me for daring to help produce another English Bible translation that started outselling even the KJV, namely, the NIV. A few of them even wrote threatening letters to me, informing me that the NIV was inspired by Satan himself from the pits of hell and warning me that I may soon be consigned there.

Second, some well-known anti-inclusive language (which to us translators means anti-gender-accurate language) Christian leaders publicly denounced and criticized CBT (which, of course, included me), IBS, and Zondervan for producing the TNIV (Today's NIV)—in spite of the fact that several popular inclusive-language versions were already circulating widely (such as the New Living Translation, the New Revised Standard Version, the New Century Version, the Good News Translation, and the Contemporary English Version) and in spite of the fact that the NIV would continue to be published as is (at least that was the plan at that time). What increased the mental and emotional anguish even more was the fact that several of these conservative-evangelical critics were personal friends of mine. I have corresponded with a few of these leaders. Here are selected paragraphs from my responses to them:

> First, I want to assure you of my prayers for you and your ministry [by which I did not mean imprecatory prayers!].
>
> The problem is that you and others refuse to recognize two facts that the rest of us do recognize: (1) The judicious, balanced use of gender-accurate language has no necessary connection at all with radical feminism and the whole egalitarian movement; (2) the generic use of masculine nouns and pronouns is rapidly dropping in the English of the 21st century. One proof of the latter is that even in many conservative-evangelical schools, publishing companies, and other institutions, their writers and editors are now being instructed to avoid the generic use of masculine terms. Most speakers and preachers today, when reading non-inclusive Scripture, will say things like: (1) The text says "men" here, but it is generic and thus includes women, so we could translate it "men and women" or "human beings" or "people"; (2) the psalm says "Blessed is the man," but "man" is generic, so we could render it "man or woman" or "person"; (3) when Paul says "brothers" here, he is addressing the whole congregation, including women, so we could say "brothers and sisters," etc., etc. And most modern speakers and writers use the singular or indefinite "they/their/them"

abundantly instead of "hc/his/him" (e.g., in sentences like "No one really knows what *they* may face in the future").

Doubtless what you are doing will cause some minor and temporary (but not irreparable) damage to IBS and Zondervan and will probably, at least to some extent and for a while, sully the good reputation of the members of CBT. But the time always comes when, having exhausted all attempts at conciliation, people must simply proceed to do what they believe God's will is for them and their ministry. In my opinion, that time has finally arrived for IBS, Zondervan, and CBT. And in the long run, I am totally convinced that God will honor and bless us for what we are doing and that his word, work, will, church, and kingdom will be enhanced and further advanced because of it.

I am glad you raised the issue of whether women actually feel excluded by all the generic masculine nouns and pronouns, because I can address it with a test case out of my own experience. A few years ago, three or four somewhat elderly Christian ladies in my church (a conservative-evangelical [not "moderate"] Southern Baptist Church) asked me what the controversy over gender language in Bible translation was all about. After I explained it to their satisfaction, out of curiosity I asked them if they really felt included in all those generic masculine terms in the Bible. To my great surprise and amazement, these conservative Christian women (uninfluenced by feminism and egalitarianism) all answered no—they did not feel included! Times have changed, and so has the English language of the 21st century, particularly with respect to the use (or, perhaps more precisely, *non-use*) of generic masculine terms—and doubly so for the younger generation we are trying to reach.

I must also take a moment to address your strong emphasis on masculinity and the so-called "male component" in certain words, particularly in Hebrew and Greek words for "man." According to the Hebrew and Greek lexicons, the primary component in Hebrew *'adam* and Greek *anthropos* is not maleness but humanness, for the first and primary definition of both terms is not "man" but "human being." So unless we render these terms as "human being(s)," at least in most contexts, we lose the *human* component that the lexicons say these words have.

I join you in praying that God's people can preserve a civil and charitable dialogue concerning this complex and contentious issue. And I applaud the efforts of those who are encouraging all parties to stop using inflammatory rhetoric, as well as to stop using terms incorrectly. I, for one, would welcome a truce. I certainly do not enjoy having to devote so much of my time and energy to correcting and clarifying all the misinformation, misrepresentations, and misconceptions now being circulated. One such misrepresentation even appeared in the March 27, 2002, issue of *USA Today*, where one of our anti-inclusive language critics was quoted as saying that muting "the masculinity intended by the authors of Scripture" violates the Gospel by "*obscuring the fatherhood of God...and the true identity of Jesus Christ.*" That statement can be misleading. Let me tell you how conservative Christians are interpreting that language. I have had several people confront me and ask, "What's this I hear

> about your Bible revision turning the Father into Mother and the Son into Child?" Of course, nothing could be further from the truth. In the TNIV [as well as in the 2011 edition of the NIV], God is still Father (not Father and Mother, or Parent), and Jesus is still the Son of God (not Child of God).
>
> I have discovered that if I take the time and energy to explain to sincere, open-minded inquirers what we are really doing (instead of what they have heard or read through various forms of the media), most of them have no problem with it at all. To us, we are simply being gender accurate. Please be assured of my prayers that the Lord will continue to bless the good work you are doing and will use your ministry for his glory and for blessing and helping others.

I close this section with the observation that when it is clear in the context that masculine terms are being used in a generic way, it is not a distortion of the meaning to use gender-accurate language. Rather, such a use makes the sense clearer to all readers, including those who are not accustomed to generic usage.

For more information on the 2011 NIV, see my article, "Updating the *New International Version* (NIV)" (Appendix 4).

Third, there was the time in the mid-1970's when I nearly landed at the bottom of John Bunyan's Slough of Despond (see his *Pilgrim's Progress*). It seemed that Murphy's Law was in full operation: "If anything can go wrong, it will." For instance, we had a fire in our house that did over $10,000 in damages. Due to destruction from a severe thunderstorm with strong winds and hail, we needed a new roof and fence. Our air conditioner broke down. We needed some expensive auto repairs. Our house was burglarized. One of our children was involved in a serious auto accident. Another had major open-heart surgery. We were experiencing some typical (but thankfully, as is turned out, only temporary) teenage problems with our children. And we had six close relatives who were having various problems. From my finite perspective nothing was going right, and everything was going wrong.

All this finally got to me, and it seemed as if Psalm 46:2-3 was happening to me spiritually and figuratively: The earth was giving way, and the mountains were falling into the heart of the sea; its waters were roaring and foaming, and the mountains were quaking with their surging. I thought my whole world was crashing down all around me. My sentiments were also similar to those of Jonah when he was drowning in the Mediterranean Sea: "You hurled me into the depths, into the very heart of the seas, and the currents swirled about me; all your waves and breakers swept over me. I said, 'I have been banished from your sight…' The engulfing waters threatened me, the deep surrounded me; seaweed was wrapped around my head. To the roots of the mountains I sank down; the earth beneath barred me in forever" (Jonah 2:3-6). I became so disappointed, discouraged, desperate, despondent, and even bitter against God that I actually contemplated resigning from my teaching position at Dallas Seminary and seeking a post where I could teach ancient Near Eastern languages, literatures, history, and religions at the doctoral level in a secular university.

How did I emerge victorious from that Slough of Despond? First, my dear wife, Isabelle, lovingly reminded me of how ridiculous such contemplations (just mentioned) were. Second, Floyd Sharp, an elder at Irving Bible Church, where I had recently served as interim pastor for a year and a half, somehow sensed that something was not quite right with me. So he kept sending me cards with words of encouragement and calling me by phone to encourage me. Here is what he wrote on two of the cards: (1) "In the recent issue of *Kindred*

Spirit magazine [published by Dallas Seminary] I saw this handsome dude with long sideburns featured in Postscript Personality. So as a result of seeing my friend and ex-pastor written up, I wanted to write and say I am thinking of and praying for the Barker family. Remember, a merry heart does good like a medicine, but a broken spirit [which is what I had at the time] dries up the bones (cf. Prov. 17:22). Anxiety in the heart of man weighs it down, but a good word makes it glad (Prov. 12:25). My good word is: "I appreciate you and your work." (2) "God loves you and is using you in a mighty way. You are special! You are appreciated! You are prayed for to have a sweet walk with our Lord and Savior. Bounty of blessings!" He stuck a smiley face on this one.

Third, God overwhelmed me with a profound sense of his persistent love, grace, faithfulness, patience, mercy, and forgiveness. I was deeply conscious of God's "love that will not let me go." In his grand old hymn, George Matheson put it like this:

> O Love that will not let me go,
> I rest my weary soul in Thee.
> I give Thee back the life I owe,
> That in Thine ocean depths its flow
> May richer, fuller be.

Because of my "restoration," my life did become "richer" and "fuller."

Fourth, I had an experience similar to that of Jeremiah. Because of pressures far greater than mine, he too wanted to quit serving the Lord (Jeremiah 20:7-18). But he couldn't! His words are also mine: "If I say, 'I will not mention his word or speak anymore in his name,' his word is in my heart like a fire, a fire shut up in my bones. I am weary of holding it in; indeed, I cannot" (Jeremiah 20:9). And so, because of the aforementioned four reasons, I emerged victorious from Bunyan's Slough of Despond by God's grace—but only after the Lord brought me to the point where I also had to acknowledge the truth of his declaration in Isaiah 55:8-9:

> "My thoughts are not your thoughts,
> neither are your ways my ways.
> As the heavens are higher than the earth,
> so are my ways higher than your ways
> and my thoughts than your thoughts."

Hindsight is better than foresight. At the time, it was a mentally and emotionally painful ordeal, and I was miserable. But as I look back on it now, I thank God for it because he used it to make me a better person. As a result, I am more humble, open, and vulnerable; more sympathetic and empathetic; more understanding, compassionate, and caring. Through it all, the Lord has given me a stronger faith and greater faithfulness and commitment. As I read somewhere: "Circumstances do not make us what we are; they reveal what we are" (see Philippians 4:11). James has an appropriate and timely word for all beleaguered believers: "Consider it pure joy, my brothers and sisters, whenever you face trials of many kinds." Why consider it pure joy? The answer comes in the next verse: "because you know that the testing of your faith produces perseverance. Let perseverance finish its work so that you may be mature and complete, not lacking anything" (James 1:2-4). And the great apostle Paul reminds us: "I consider that our present sufferings are not worth comparing with the glory that will be revealed in us" (Romans 8:18). He adds: "Therefore we do not lose heart. Though outwardly we are wasting away, yet inwardly we are being renewed day by day. For our light and momentary troubles are achieving for us an eternal glory that far outweighs them all. So we fix our eyes not on what is seen, but on what is unseen, since what is seen is temporary, but what is unseen is eternal" (2 Corinthians 4:16-18).

Why have I devoted considerable space to the episode concerning this low point in my life and ministry? Because of the manner in which God has already used this story when I have shared it with others. In my preaching and teaching ministry, I have occasionally shared this experience in large conferences. Invariably, several have come up afterward to thank me for encouraging them in this way. They have said things like: "Thank you for being open and vulnerable enough to share your story with us. That's exactly where we are. Because of your encouraging word, we plan to hang in there and persevere in faith, faithfulness, fruitfulness, and obedience to God's will as revealed in his Word." Now my prayer is that the Lord will similarly use this written form of my story to encourage numerous other believers.

So I can identify with David's thoughts in Psalm 13:

> 1 How long, Lord? Will you forget me forever?
> How long will you hide your face from me?
> 2 How long must I wrestle with my thoughts
> and day after day have sorrow in my heart?
> How long will my enemy triumph over me?
> 3 Look on me and answer, Lord my God.
> Give light to my eyes, or I will sleep in death,
> 4 and my enemy will say, "I have overcome him,"
> and my foes will rejoice when I fall.
>
> 5 But I trust in your unfailing love;
> my heart rejoices in your salvation.
> 6 I will sing the Lord's praise,
> for he has been good to me.

Through all the vicissitudes of life, God "has been good to me." Yes, God <u>is</u> good <u>all</u> the time (in spite of the bad days!). Many years ago, I heard someone say, "Never doubt in the dark what God has shown you in the light." One of the things God has shown you in the light is that he is good. So never doubt that fact when the dark times come.

Another important verse on this theme is Genesis 50:20, where Joseph tells his brothers, "You intended to harm me, but God intended it for good to accomplish what is now being done, the saving of many lives." One of my two life passages is Romans 8:28-30 (the other one is Philippians 1:20-21 [quoted in Chapter Eight]): "And we know that in all things God works for the good of those who love him, who have been called according to his purpose. For those God foreknew he also predestined to be conformed to the image of his Son, that he might be the firstborn among many brothers and sisters. And those he predestined, he also called; those he called, he also justified; those he justified, he also glorified [note the past tense—it is as good as done!]." In my spiritual pilgrimage this passage has greatly encouraged me on numerous occasions. A recurring theme in Scripture is: "Give thanks to the Lord, for he is good, his [faithful] love endures forever" (1 Chronicles 16:34; see also Psalms 106:1; 107:1; 118:1, 29; 136:1).

George Mueller (in [Mrs.] L.B. Cowman's *Streams in the Desert*, Zondervan, 1997, pages 156-157) gives us this word on God's goodness:

> *I trust in your word.* (Psalm 119:42)
>
> The strength of our faith is in direct proportion to our level of belief that God will do exactly what He has promised. Faith has nothing to do with feelings, impressions, outward appearances, nor the probability or improbability of an event. If we try to couple these things with faith, we are no longer resting on the Word of God, because faith is not dependent on them. *Faith rests on the pure Word of God alone.* And when we take Him at His Word, our hearts are at peace.
>
> God delights in causing us to exercise our faith. He does so to bless us individually, to bless the

church at large, and as a witness to unbelievers. Yet we tend to retreat from the exercising of our faith instead of welcoming it. When trials come, our response should be, "My heavenly Father has placed this cup of trials into my hands so I may later have something pleasant."

Trials are the food of faith. Oh, may we leave ourselves in the hands of our heavenly Father! It is the joy of His heart to do good to all His children. Yet trials and difficulties are not the only way faith is exercised and thereby increased. *Reading the Scriptures also acquaints us with God as He has revealed Himself in them.*

Are you able to genuinely say, from your knowledge of God and your relationship with Him, that he is indeed a beautiful Being? If not, let me graciously encourage you to ask God to take you to that point, so you will fully appreciate His gentleness and kindness, so you will be able to say just how good He is, and so you will know what a delight it is to God's heart to do good for His children.

The closer we come to this point in our inner being, the more willing we are to leave ourselves in His hands and the more satisfied we are with all of His dealings with us. Then when trials come, we will say, "I will patiently wait to see the good that God will do in my life, with the calm assurance He will do it."

In this way, we will bear a worthy testimony to the world and thereby strengthen the lives of others.

One of my favorite paintings is by Warner Sallman—given to me by my dear wife (Isabelle) to hang on the wall of my study/office. It pictures a man in a small boat on a storm-tossed sea in an obviously life-threatening situation, but it also shows Christ in the boat with him—guiding, helping, and protecting him (cf. Mark 4:35-41). When I experience some of the storms of life, I recall that painting, which, in turn, reminds me of the words of Edward Hopper:

Jesus, Savior, pilot me
Over life's tempestuous sea:
Unknown waves before me roll,
Hiding rocks and treach'rous shoal;
Chart and compass come from Thee—
Jesus Savior, pilot me!

When at last I near the shore,
And the fearful breakers roar
'Twixt me and the peaceful rest—
Then, while leaning on Thy breast,
May I hear Thee say to me,
"Fear not—I will pilot thee!"

Similar words come from H.L. Gilmour:

I've anchored my soul in the haven of rest,
I'll sail the wide seas no more;
The tempest may sweep o'er the wild, stormy deep,
In Jesus I'm safe evermore.

I close with a selection of more of my favorite poetic stanzas on the general theme, "God is good all the time (in spite of the bad days)," starting with one of my favorite hymns, "My Jesus, I Love Thee":

William R. Featherston:

My Jesus, I love Thee; I know Thou art mine;

For Thee all the follies of sin I resign.
My gracious Redeemer, my Savior art Thou;
If ever I loved Thee, my Jesus, 'tis now.

I love Thee because Thou hast first loved me
And purchased my pardon on Calvary's tree,
I love Thee for wearing the thorns on Thy brow;
If ever I loved Thee, my Jesus, 'tis now.

I'll love Thee in life; I will love Thee in death
And praise Thee as long as Thou lendest me breath,
And say when the death-dew lies cold on my brow,
"If ever I loved Thee, my Jesus, 'tis now."

In mansions of glory and endless delight,
I'll ever adore Thee in heaven so bright,
I'll sing with the glittering crown on my brow,
"If ever I loved Thee, my Jesus, 'tis now."

John Newton:

The Lord has promised good to me,
His word my hope secures;
He will my shield and portion be
As long as life endures.

William Cowper:

(1)
God moves in a mysterious way
His wonders to perform;
He plants His footsteps in the sea
and rides upon the storm.

(5)

Blind unbelief is sure to err
        and scan His work in vain;
God is His own interpreter,
        and He will make it plain.

Grant Colfax Tullar:

The Weaver

My life is but a weaving
        Between my Lord and me;
I cannot choose the colors
        He worketh steadily.

Ofttimes He weaveth sorrow,
        And I in foolish pride
Forget He sees the upper
        And I, the underside.

Not till the loom is silent
        And the shuttles cease to fly
Shall God unroll the canvas
        And explain the reason why.

The dark threads are as needful
        In the Weaver's skillful hand
As the threads of gold and silver
        In the pattern He has planned.

Annie Johnson Flint:

What God Hath Promised

God hath not promised skies always blue,
Flower-strewn pathways all our lives through;
God hath not promised sun without rain,
Joy without sorrow, peace without pain.
God hath not promised we shall not know

Toil and temptation, trouble and woe;
He hath not told us we shall not bear
Many a burden, many a care.

God hath not promised smooth roads and wide,
Swift, easy travel, needing no guide;
Never a mountain, rocky and steep,
Never a river, turbid and deep.

But God hath promised strength for the day,
Rest for the labor, light for the way,
Grace for the trials, help from above,
Unfailing sympathy, undying love.

Brother Lawrence:

Good when He gives, supremely good,
Nor less when He denies;
Afflictions, from His sovereign hand,
Are blessings in disguise.

E. Margaret Clarkson:

He Knows

He knows it all—the winding path,
    The sky o'ercast and grey,
The steepness of the mountainside,
    The roughness of the way.

He knows it all—the haunting fear,
    The doubtings that distress,
The wond'rings and perplexities,
    And all the strain and stress.

He knows it all—each troubled thought,
    Each anxious wave of care,
And every burden, every grief,

Or cross that thou must bear.
He knows it all—thy weight of woe,
Thine often tear-dimmed eye,
The stabbing pain, the slow, dull ache,
And sorrow's broken cry.

He knows it all—but His to choose,
And thine to take His choice!
He knows it all! He planned it so!
Then trust Him, and rejoice!

John Greenleaf Whittier:

The Eternal Goodness

I see the wrong that round me lies,
I feel the guilt within;
I hear, with groan and travail-cries,
The world confess its sin.

Yet in the maddening maze of things,
And tossed by storm and flood,
To one fixed trust my spirit clings:
I know that God is good!

Cleaver of Egypt (a good epitaph for one's whole life):

When my life is past,
how glad I shall be
that the lamp of my life
has been shining for Thee.

I shall then not regret what I gave
of labor or money for sinners to save.
I shall not mind
that the way has been rough.
That my Savior led me—
that will be enough.
When I am dying,

how glad I shall be
that the lamp of my life
has been shining for Thee.

Unknown:

And shall I use these ransomed powers of mine
For things that only minister to me?
Lord, take my tongue, my hands, my heart, my all,
And let me live and love and give for Thee.

Tommy Walker:

We Will Remember

You're our creator, our life sustainer,
Deliverer, our comfort, our joy;
Throughout the ages You've been our shelter,
Our peace in the midst of the storm.

With signs and wonders You've shown Your power,
With precious blood You showed us Your grace;
You've been our helper, our liberator,
The giver of life with no end.

When we walk though life's darkest valleys,
We will look back at all You have done;
And we will shout, our God is good,
And He is the faithful One.

<u>Bridge</u>
Hallelujah, hallelujah,
To the one from whom all blessings flow;
Hallelujah, hallelujah,
To the one whose glory has been shown.

I still remember the day You saved me,
The day I heard You call out my name;

You said You loved me and would never leave me,
And I've never been the same.

<u>Chorus</u>
We will remember, we will remember,
We will remember the works of Your hands;
We will stop and give You praise,
For great is Thy faithfulness.

Yes, "great is your faithfulness" (Lamentations 3:23).

The race of Christian life and service is not a short sprint. As someone has put it, "Christian experience is not to be an initial spasm followed by a chronic inertia." Rather, the Christian race is a marathon, so we need to heed the words of W.A. Ogden (penned in 1885) and follow Jesus "<u>all the way</u>":

W.A. Ogden:

Where He Leads I'll Follow
(1)
Sweet are the promises, Kind is the word,
Dearer far than any message man ever heard;
Pure was the mind of Christ, Sinless I see;
He the great example is, and pattern for me.

(3)
List to His loving words, "Come unto Me";
Weary, heavy-laden, there is sweet rest for thee;
Trust in His promises, Faithful and sure;
Lean upon the Savior, and thy soul is secure.

<u>Chorus</u>
Where He leads I'll follow, Follow all the way;
Where He leads I'll follow, Follow Jesus every day.

And, finally, an anonymous writer accurately captures my

closing sentiments:

> When the storm is raging high,
> When the tempest rends the sky,
> When my eyes with tears are dim,
> Then, my soul, consider Him.
>
> When my plans are in the dust,
> When my dearest hopes are crushed,
> When is passed each foolish whim,
> Then, my soul, consider Him.
>
> When I track my weary way,
> When fresh trials come each day,
> When my faith and hope are dim,
> Then, my soul, consider Him.
>
> Clouds or sunshine, dark or bright,
> Evening shades or morning light,
> When my cup flows o'er the brim,
> Then, my soul, consider Him.

So God is good all the time (in spite of the bad days)! Yes, the Lord has certainly brought me a long way since those early days as a barefoot boy wearing only overalls with galluses in the hills of southeastern Kentucky. It shows what our extraordinary God can accomplish through ordinary humans. My feelings are the same as David's in 2 Samuel 7:18: "Who am I, Sovereign LORD, and what is my family, that you have brought me this far?" I also fully concur with the psalmist who wrote in Psalm 119:68: "You are good, and what you do is good."

My closing prayer:

> Father, may everything I do and say contribute to bringing greater glory to you, because you alone deserve all the credit, thanks, praise, honor, and glory. I exist for you. I don't want others to see my good deeds and glorify me. Rather, I want them to see the good that you have enabled me to accomplish and glorify you. You have been so good to me and blessed me with so many good things that I want to praise you forever for your goodness. In the name of, and for the glory of, your Son and my Savior and Lord, Jesus Christ, Amen.

"By the grace of God I am what I am."

APPENDIX 1

DR. KENNETH BARKER
Biographical Sketch

Dr. Kenneth Barker is an author and speaker living in Lewisville, Texas. Until his retirement from International Bible Society (now Biblica) in 1996, he was Executive Director of their NIV Translation Center. He was also one of the original translators of the *New International Version* of the Bible and a regular spokesperson for its Committee on Bible Translation—the governing body that produced the NIV.

Ken Barker has given talks about the translation process of the NIV all over the U.S. and abroad, and much of his time is spent writing, editing, preaching, and teaching. He also worked on the *New International Reader's Version* (a simplification of the NIV for those who read at a lower reading level), three books about the NIV and *The NIV Study Bible* as its General Editor.

Ken Barker and his wife, Isabelle, have four children—Ken, Patricia, Ruth, and David—and 29 grandchildren, including 9 great-grandchildren and 1 great-great-grandson. The Barkers worship and serve at First Baptist Church of Carrollton, Texas. In his spare time, Ken enjoys music, reading, table tennis (ping-pong), swimming, walking, and, for leisure, watching news, weather, and sports on TV; he also enjoys reading the newspaper..

He holds the B.A. degree from Northwestern College, the Th.M. from Dallas Theological Seminary, and the Ph.D. from the Dropsie College for Hebrew and Cognate Learning. He has served as Academic Dean of Capital Bible Seminary, Professor of Old Testament at three theological seminaries (including Dallas Theological Seminary for 13 years) and Visiting Professor at two others. He is also author of commentaries on the books of Micah and Zechariah, as well as co-editor of the *Expositor's Bible Commentary* (Abridged Edition, 2 volumes).

Most recently he has helped produce the 2011 edition of the NIV and the 2011 *NIV Study Bible* as its General Editor.

APPENDIX 2

PERSONALIA

(Primarily Academic) on Dr. Kenneth L. Barker
Author and Speaker
Lewisville, TX

EDUCATIONAL BACKGROUND

B.A., 1955, Northwestern College; Th.M., 1960, Dallas Theological Seminary; Ph.D., 1969, The Dropsie College for Hebrew and Cognate Learning.

VOCATIONAL EXPERIENCE

Teaching Fellow, 1962-64, Dropsie College; Instructor and Chairman, Biblical Studies and Philosophy, 1964-66, Northwestern College; Assistant Professor, Old Testament and Archaeology, 1966-68, Trinity Evangelical Divinity School; Professor and Chairman, Semitics and Old Testament Studies, 1968-81, and Adjunct Teacher, 2001, Dallas Theological Seminary; Executive Secretary, 1981-87, NIV Committee on Bible Translation; Senior Vice President, 1981-86, International Bible Society; Academic Dean, 1986-90, Capital Bible Seminary; Executive Director, NIV Translation Center (a ministry of International Bible Society), 1990-96 (retired).

PUBLICATIONS

Primary publications: author, *Micah*, New American Commentary (Broadman & Holman); general editor, *The NIV Study Bible* (Zondervan); author, "Zechariah," in *Expositor's Bible Commentary* (Zondervan); editor, *Expositor's Bible Commentary: Abridged Edition*; author, "The Scope and Center of Old and New Testament Theology and Hope," in *Dispensationalism, Israel and the Church* (Zondervan); author, "Evidence from Daniel," in *A Case for Premillennialism* (Moody); author, "Premillennialism in the Book of Daniel," in The *Master's Perspective on Biblical Prophecy* (Kregel); author, "Praise," in *Cracking Old Testament Codes: A Guide to Interpreting the Literary Genres of the Old Testament* (Broadman & Holman); author, "Hearing God's Word Through a Good Translation," in *Reading and Hearing the Word: From Text to Sermon* (CRC Publications); general editor, *Wycliffe Exegetical Commentary* (Moody); consulting editor for the Old Testament, *The Bible Knowledge Commentary* (Victor); co-translator, *The New American Standard Bible*; co-translator and co-editor; *Holy Bible: New International Version* (several publishers); co-translator and co-editor, *Holy Bible: Today's New International Version*; editor, *The Making of the NIV* (Baker); author, *The Accuracy of the NIV* and *The Balance of the NIV* (Baker); Scripture editor and theological consultant, *The Hymnal for Worship and Celebration* (Word), *Songs for Praise and Worship* (Word), and *The Celebration Hymnal* (Integrity &Word); member of Theology Committee, *Baptist Hymnal* and *Worship Hymnal* (LifeWay).

Additional publications: author, "The Antiquity and Historicity of the Patriarchal Narratives," in *A Tribute to Gleason Archer* (Moody); author, "A Response to Historical-Grammatical Problems," in *Hermeneutics, Inerrancy, and the Bible* (Zondervan); author, "Jeremiah's Ministry and Ours," in *Vital Ministry Issues* (Kregel); author, "Bible Translation Philosophies with Special Reference to the NIV," in *The Challenge of Bible Translation* (Zondervan); author,

"Introduction" to reprint of *Israel and the Aramaeans of Damascus* (Baker) by M.F. Unger; author, "Foreword" to *The Servant Songs* (Moody) by F.D. Lindsey; author, "Foreword" to *A Biblical Theology of the Old Testament* (Moody) edited by R.B. Zuck; author, "Foreword" to *English Language Bible Translators* (McFarland) by W.E. Paul; co-author, "Foreword" to *Index to Brown, Driver and Briggs Hebrew Lexicon* (Moody) compiled by B. Einspahr; author, articles and book reviews in *Journal of Biblical Literature, Journal of the Evangelical Theological Society, The Master's Seminary Journal, Zondervan Pictorial Encyclopedia of the Bible, Wycliffe Bible Encyclopedia, Baker Encyclopedia of the Bible, Hebrew Studies, Bibliotheca Sacra, Moody Monthly, Christian Herald, Kindred Spirit, Bookstore Journal, Charisma, Journal of the Ancient Near Eastern Society*, and *Bible Editions and Versions.*

HONORS

All graduations have been with distinction or high honor; selected as a Fellow of Dropsie College; present or past member of the National Association of Professors of Hebrew, Near East Archaeological Society, National Association of Evangelicals, the Committee on Bible Translation of the *New International Version* and the Final Review Committee of the *New International Reader's Version*, the Society of Biblical Literature, and the American Oriental Society; President of the Evangelical Theological Society, 1981; Distinguished Alumnus of Northwestern College of 1988.

CHURCH MINISTRY

Currently senior deacon and teacher, First Baptist Church, Carrollton, TX; Interim Pastor, Rusk Bethel Baptist Church, Menomonie, WI, 1964-65; Riverside Evangelical Free Church, Minneapolis, MN, 1965-66; Irving Bible Church, Irving, TX, 1971-73; Lubbock Bible Church, Lubbock, TX, 1980; Alliance Church, Cranford, NJ, 1983; and Faith Evangelical Free Church, Freehold, NJ, 1985-86;

presently conducts preaching and teaching ministries also in various churches and schools.

TRAVELS

Andorra, Austria, Belgium, Canada, Crete, Czech Republic, England, France, Germany, Greece, Holland, Hungary, Ireland (both Northern and the Republic), Israel, Italy, Luxembourg, Mallorca, Mexico, Nigeria, Portugal, Scotland, Spain, Wales and all fifty states of the U.S.A.

APPENDIX 3

Action of CBT at its June 19, 2004, meeting in Elk Grove Village, IL:

On behalf of CBT the Chair thanks Ken Barker for his long-time invaluable service as Secretary of CBT. After joining CBT in the summer of 1974, Ken was elected to serve as the Committee's Secretary already on January 4, 1975, and from that time to the present his name has stood at the conclusion of every set of Minutes of CBT's plenary meetings—indicating a remarkable 30 years of service, much longer than the incumbency of any other member of CBT's Executive Committee. This record provides clear testimony of Ken's unflagging devotion to CBT's mission. It also bears witness to CBT's continued high evaluation of his services. The work of Secretary entailed more than the recording of matters dealt with in CBT's annual "business" meetings. It was the Secretary's responsibility also to keep the official record of all of CBT's translation and editorial decisions, a task that Ken fulfilled with unerring accuracy. Although not inherently the Secretary's responsibility, after the death of Dr. Edwin Palmer, CBT asked Ken on November 1, 1980, to take on also the task of Executive Secretary, a task he carried out until December 31, 1987. As a result, it fell to him to perform the extremely demanding function of chairing CBT's translation and editorial sessions. In this role, Ken's remarkable powers of recall, his congeniality, patience, even-handedness and sense of humor, his sensitivity to proper grammar, his matchless attention to detail and his physical stamina became so evident that CBT has asked him to continue to serve in this capacity up to the present. Without his unique contribution in chairing its work sessions, CBT could not have functioned as efficiently or with the cohesion that it has. And to this must be added the indispensable contribution Ken has made to the proofreading of the keyed text of both the NIV and TNIV. No detail, however minute, escapes his eye, so that the virtually errorless printed text is (and will be) largely the result of his careful scrutiny of the page proofs. CBT owes much to its long serving Secretary, Ken Barker.

Note could also be taken of still other contributions Ken has made to CBT's translation projects, his travels, speeches, correspondence and publications on behalf of the NIV and TNIV, but these do not pertain directly to his role as Secretary. CBT would be seriously remiss, however, if it did not acknowledge with deep gratitude, the essential contribution of the Secretary's secretary. In the midst of all the demands of her already busy life, Ken's wife Isabelle has found the time and energy to transcribe all of Ken's handwritten materials into accurate typescript. Her devotion to the work of CBT has been no less and no less enduring than her husband's. CBT thanks you, Isabelle.

APPENDIX 4

UPDATING THE *NEW INTERNATIONAL VERSION* (NIV)

Dr. Kenneth L. Barker
(General Editor, *NIV Study Bible*, 2011)

Probably most Bible readers know that 2011 marks the 400th anniversary of the King James Version (KJV), or Authorized Version (AV), of the Bible. Biblica (formerly International Bible Society and the holder of the copyright to the NIV) and Zondervan (the primary publisher of commercial editions of the NIV) decided that one way they wanted to help celebrate the KJV's 400th anniversary was to produce a 2011 update of the 1984 NIV. They then asked the NIV Committee on Bible Translation (CBT), on which I served, to revise (or improve—my preferred term) the current NIV for such a 2011 edition, and it was released to the general public in early 2011.

How is the 2011 NIV different from the 1984 NIV, as well as from the TNIV? A few of the differences are delineated in the Preface:

> One of the shifts [in English] that creates particular challenges…is the manner in which

> gender is presented... This [2011] edition ..., along with almost all other recent English translations, substitutes other expressions when the original text intends to refer generically to men and women equally. Thus, for instance, the 1984 NIV rendering of 1 Corinthians 8:3, "But the man who loves God is known by God," becomes in this edition, "But whoever loves God is known by God." On the other hand, "man" and "mankind," as ways of denoting the human race, are still widely used. This edition of the NIV therefore continues to use these words, along with other expressions, in this way.

Concerning the use of the singular/indefinite "they/them/their," the Preface explains:

> A related shift in English creates a greater challenge for modern translations: the move away from using the third-person masculine singular pronouns – "he/him/his" – to refer to men and women equally. This usage does persist... in some forms of English, and this revision therefore occasionally uses these pronouns in a generic sense. But the tendency, recognized in day-to-day usage and confirmed by extensive research, is away from the generic use of "he," "him" and "his." In recognition of this shift ... and in an effort to translate into the "common" English that people are actually using, this revision ... generally uses other constructions when the biblical text is plainly addressed to men and women equally. The reader will frequently encounter a "they," "them" or "their" to express a generic singular idea. Thus, for instance, Mark 8:36 reads: "What good is it for someone to gain the whole world, yet forfeit their soul?" This generic use of the "indefinite"

> or "singular" "they/them/their" has a venerable place in English idiom and has quickly become established as standard English … all over the world. Where an individual emphasis is deemed to be present, "anyone" or "everyone" or some other equivalent is generally used as the antecedent of such pronouns.

Prior to this 2011 update of the NIV, all previous Bible translation efforts had been hampered by the lack of accurate, statistically significant data on the state of spoken and written English at a given time in its history. Translators and stylists had to rely on their own subjective experiences and judgments. CBT sought to remove some of this subjectivity by initiating a relationship with Collins Dictionaries in order to use the Collins Bank of English, one of the world's foremost English language research tools, as a guide for gender language. Their Bank of English is a database of more than 4.4 billion words drawn from text publications and spoken-word recordings from all over the world. So CBT gained an authoritative, and hitherto unavailable, perspective on the contemporary use of gender language. The study examined gender language in English in three specific areas of usage over a 20-year period from 1990 to 2009:

> (1) Generic pronouns: masculine generic pronouns (such as "he"), expressed as a percentage of total generic pronoun usage in general written English, fell from 22 percent to 8 percent. For example, it became more and more common to follow singular antecedents like "someone," "whoever," "everyone," "person" and "individual" with "they."
> (2) Mankind, man and synonyms: Here the most common terms employed were "people," "humans," "man," "humanity" and "mankind." The 2011 NIV uses all these.
> (3) Forefather and ancestor: "Ancestor" is significantly more frequent than "forefather."

Before leaving the subject of gender language, it is important to emphasize that every single change introduced into CBT's last major revision (the TNIV) relating to inclusive language for humanity was reconsidered. Some results of such reconsiderations were: (1) Using plurals instead of singulars to deal with generic forms (as in the TNIV) was avoided; (2) using second-person forms instead of third-person forms to deal with generics (as in the TNIV) was avoided; (3) "brothers and sisters" instead of just "brothers" was used to translate the Greek word *adelphoi* when it was clear that both genders were in view (*adelphoi* is also used in the sense of "brothers and sisters" in Greek literature outside the New Testament in New Testament times). When *adelphoi* is used in this generic sense, its first occurrence in a book is footnoted in the following way: "The Greek word for *brothers and sisters* (*adelphoi*) refers here to believers, both men and women, as part of God's family; also in ..." (here the other references in that book are given). For example, see the footnote to Romans 1:13. Actually we have added several new, helpful, explanatory footnotes. Another one is on our use of the word "flesh" most of the time in place of "sinful nature" for Greek *sarx*. For instance, Romans 7:5 now reads "For when we were in the realm of the flesh, ..." (instead of the 1984 rendering, "For when we were controlled by the sinful nature, ... "), with this footnote: "In contexts like this, the Greek word for *flesh* (*sarx*) refers to the sinful state of human beings, often presented as a power in opposition to the Spirit."

In order to avoid the erroneous notion that the 2011 NIV is *substantially* different from the 1984 NIV, it must be stressed that about 95 percent of the text of the updated NIV is exactly the *same* as the *1984* text it replaces! A few of the reasons for changing (improving) about 5 percent of the text included (1) changes in English (e.g., "foreigner" instead of "alien"), (2) progress in scholarship (e.g., using "rebels" instead of "robbers" in Mark 15:27), and (3) concern for greater clarity (we improved the clarity of numerous passages).

Finally, here is a small selection of new (different from the 1984 NIV) renderings that to me represent improvements:

Gen. 1:26 (1984) "Let us make man…, and let them rule…."
(2011) "Let us make mankind…, so that they may rule…."

Deut. 10:21 (1984) "He is your praise."
(2011) "He is the one you praise" (similarly Ps. 22:3; Jer. 17:14).

Josh. 1:8 (1984) "Do not let this Book of the Law depart from your mouth."
(2011) "Keep this Book of the Law always on your lips" (similarly Isa. 59:21).

Mic. 1:15 (1984) "He who is the glory of Israel will come to Adullam."
(2011) "The nobles of Israel will flee to Adullam."

Mic. 5:5-6 (1984) "And he will be their peace."

Deliverance and Destruction

"When the Assyrian invades our land
and marches through our fortresses,
we will raise against him seven shepherds,
even eight leaders of men.
They will rule the land of Assyria with the sword,
the land of Nimrod with drawn sword.
He will deliver us from the Assyrian
when he invades our land
and marches into our borders."

(2011)
"And he will be our peace [and security]
when the Assyrians invade our land
and march through our fortresses.

We will raise against them seven shepherds,
even eight commanders,
who will rule the land of Assyria with the sword,
the land of Nimrod with drawn sword.
He will deliver us from the Assyrians
when they invade our land
and march across our borders."

Zech. 4:10
(1984) "Who despises the day of small things? Men will rejoice when they see the plumb line in the hand of Zerubbabel. (These seven are the eyes of the Lord, which range throughout the earth.)"
(2011) "Who dares despise the day of small things, since the seven eyes of the Lord that range throughout the earth will rejoice when they see the chosen capstone in the hand of Zerubbabel?"

Matt. 10:29
(1984) "Are not two sparrows sold for a penny? Yet not one of them will fall to the ground apart from the will of your Father."
(2011) "Are not two sparrows sold for a penny? Yet not one of them will fall to the ground outside your Father's care."

John 4:24
(1984) "God is spirit, and his worshipers must worship in spirit and in truth."
(2011) "God is spirit, and his worshipers must worship in the Spirit and in truth."

Rom. 8:3
(1984) "And so he condemned sin in sinful man."
(2011) "And so he condemned sin in the flesh" (i.e., in Christ's human body on the cross).

Rom. 8:15

(1984) "... you received the Spirit of sonship."
(2011) "... the Spirit you received brought about your adoption to sonship." There is also a helpful explanatory footnote here: "The Greek word for *adoption to sonship* is a term referring to the full legal standing of an adopted male heir in Roman culture; also in verse 23."

Phil. 3:6
(1984) "... as for legalistic righteousness, faultless."
(2011) "as for righteousness based on the law, faultless."

1 John 2:16
(1984) "For everything in the world – the cravings of sinful man, the lust of his eyes and the boasting of what he has and does – comes not from the Father but from the world."
(2011) "For everything in the world – the lust of the flesh, the lust of the eyes, and the pride of life – comes not from the Father but from the world." Here we decided that changing the familiar language of the KJV (as we did in the 1984 edition) really did not improve the verse, so we returned to the familiar wording.

To quote from a CBT document:

"It has been a profound privilege for us as translators to return, once again, to the vision that first inspired the team who began this great work. When God spoke through the text of the Bible, he said exactly what he wanted to say in the language of everyday people. Two thousand years later, we have sought to give the world a Bible translation that reflects those same priorities: Hear God's Word the way it was written and understand it the way it was meant! Take it, read it, listen to it, pray over it, enjoy it and use it to grow in Christian maturity!"
(This article was published in *Bible Editions & Versions*, 13/1, January-March 2012, pp. 7-11.)

APPENDIX 5

Members of CBT
(NIV COMMITTEE ON BIBLE TRANSLATION)

The members of the Committee on Bible Translation (CBT) when the original NIV Bible was completed in 1978 were: Ken Barker (Dallas Theological Seminary), Ralph Earle (Nazarene Theological Seminary), Burt Goddard (Gordon-Conwell Theological Seminary), Laird Harris (Covenant Theological Seminary), Earl Kalland (Conservative Baptist Theological Seminary), Youngve Kindberg (President, New York International Bible Society, the NIV financial sponsor), Dick Longenecker (Wycliffe College, University of Toronto), Bill Martin (Regent College, Vancouver), Steve Paine (Houghton College), Robert Preus (Concordia Theological Seminary), John Stek (Calvin Theological Seminary), Larry Walker (Southwestern Baptist Theological Seminary), J. C. Wenger (Goshen Biblical Seminary), and Marten Woudstra (Calvin Theological Seminary). Ed Palmer was the Executive Secretary of CBT and Coordinator of the Translation Project. Bruce Waltke (Regent College, Vancouver) and Ron Youngblood (Bethel Theological Seminary) were also co-opted to help CBT finish the NIV in 1978.

The members of CBT when the 2011 edition of the NIV was completed were: Doug Moo, Chair (Wheaton College Graduate School), Mark Strauss, Vice-Chair (Bethel Seminary, San Diego), Karen Jobes, Secretary (Wheaton College), Ken Barker (Retired), Craig Bloomberg (Denver Seminary), Jeannine Brown (Bethel Seminary), Gordon Fee (Retired), R. T. (Dick) France (Retired), David Instone-Brewer (Tyndale House), Bill Mounce (BiblicalTraining.org), Paul Swarup, (Christ Church, Delhi), Larry Walker (Retired), Bruce Waltke (Knox Theological Seminary), Michael Williams (Calvin Theological Seminary), Ron Youngblood (Bethel Seminary, San Diego).